TRANSFORMATIONAL

LEADERSHIP

&

DECISION MAKING

in

SCHOOLS

TRANSFORMATIONAL

LEADERSHIP

$\mathcal{E}$

DECISION MAKING

in

SCHOOLS

ROBERT E. BROWER
BRADLEY V. BALCH

CORWIN PRESS
A SAGE Publications Company
Thousand Oaks, California

For information:

Corwin Press
A Sage Publications Company
2455 Teller Road
Thousand Oaks, California 91320
www.corwinpress.com

Sage Publications Ltd.
1 Oliver's Yard
55 City Road
London EC1Y 1SP
United Kingdom

Sage Publications India Pvt. Ltd.
B-42, Panchsheel Enclave
Post Box 4109
New Delhi 110 017 India

Printed in the United States of America.

Library of Congress Cataloging-in-Publication Data

Brower, Robert E.
Transformational leadership & decision making in schools / Robert E. Brower, Bradley V. Balch.
  p. cm.
Includes bibliographical references and index.
ISBN 1–4129–1486–8 (cloth)—ISBN 1–4129–1487–6 (pbk.)
   1. School management and organization—Decision making. 2. Educational leadership. I. Title: Transformational leadership and decision making in schools. II. Balch, Bradley V. III. Title.
LB2806.B794 2005
371.2—dc22   2004028753

This book is printed on acid-free paper.

05 06 07 08 09 10 9 8 7 6 5 4 3 2 1

Acquisitions Editor:	Elizabeth Brenkus
Editorial Assistant:	Candice L. Ling
Production Editor:	Laureen A. Shea
Copy Editor:	Liann Lech
Typesetter:	C&M Digitals (P) Ltd.
Proofreader:	Kevin Gleason
Indexer:	Naomi Linzer
Cover Designer:	Rose Storey
Graphic Designer:	Anthony Paular

Contents

Preface

For school leaders, effective decisions have become clouded with ever-growing uncertainty and skepticism, especially difficult decisions. Stakeholders of education maintain high expectations for accountability and expect "me-first" entitlement. In this complex environment, decisions can quickly backfire and blow up in the face of school leaders with adverse effects and unintended consequences. It appears at every juncture of decision making that school leaders are being criticized for their decisions by any one of a number of individuals or institutions, including their own employees. These criticisms and the negative environment they create can overwhelm a leader, adversely affecting decision making. Compound these oppositional forces with the loneliness often associated with decision making and untenable situations can manifest, costing a leader his or her position and creating professional and personal duress. Enormous pressures are being placed on our nation's school leaders at the building and district level. These pressures are compounded when school leaders lack a sound decision-making pedagogy, often unintentionally projected as an attempt to be *all* things to *all* people.

Transformational decision making is a framework of considerations, created to give leaders the confidence to act decisively with a sound decision-making pedagogy. Whether day-to-day decisions, or divisive and difficult decisions, leaders embracing this pedagogy will find themselves leading in profoundly positive, meaningful ways. Stakeholders of education will also benefit from a transformational perspective as the vision, mission, and overall common good permeate decisions.

Transformational decision making will not script which decisions to make, but how to make decisions by providing a framework of sound decision-making considerations. Simply stated, this pedagogy better ensures successful leadership by encouraging leaders to ask the question, "What is in the best interest of the institution I lead?" The genuine and thoughtful answer to this question requires a consistent decision-making pedagogy.

Thirteen chapters describe essential considerations for making decisions. Each chapter is predicated on decision-making leadership that is transformational in an institutional context. *Transformational decision making* means thinking and acting in ways that reflect the common good as the leadership imperative, not the individual good. *Institution* identifies the name of various school entities. This might include school corporations, schools, organizations, teams, departments, classrooms, or unions. To be considered an institution, the entity must be composed of stakeholders (i.e., a membership); have a purpose; and possess some type of formal or informal leadership (e.g., board president, superintendent, principal, teacher, coach, department chair, or spokesperson). An institution is intended to represent the common good of its stakeholders.

Armed with this understanding, the reader crafts a personal pedagogy of decision making based on essential themes that include, in part, the role of vision and mission, capacity for change, motivation, laws of nature, barriers to decision making, development of respect and rapport, empowerment and delegation, and the effects of the for-profit sector. Each chapter concludes with a conceptual framework, which includes concise, step-by-step considerations to inform the leader's decision making. Also included at the end of each chapter is a reflective thinking section, which includes several questions for individual reflection, group discussion, and team conversations. Based on the belief that great leaders ask great questions, both the conceptual framework and reflective thinking sections are immersed in a thought-provoking question format for the reader to reveal the values and beliefs associated with the decision-making considerations.

Readers are encouraged to complete the decision-making self-assessment. It is intended to establish the respondent's baseline perceptions about how to make decisions. This 40-item inventory is an essential first step toward the journey of developing a sound and effective decision-making pedagogy. When taken by multiple stakeholders, the assessment can also inform various institutions regarding their decision-making capacity.

The authors owe a great debt of gratitude to the school leaders who generously shared their wisdom, real-life stories, and testimonials. Their passion, enthusiasm, and commitment to the noble profession of education made the development of this book a truly rewarding experience.

Acknowledgments

T he authors and Corwin Press gratefully acknowledge the contributions of the following individuals:

Randel Beaver
Superintendent
Archer City Independent School District
Archer City, TX

Frank Bush
Executive Director
Indiana School Boards Association
Indianapolis, IN

Harriet Gould
Principal
Raymond Central Elementary School
Valparaiso, NE

James Halley
Superintendent of Schools
North Kingstown School District
North Kingstown, RI

Kay Harmless
Interim Director
Indiana Principal Leadership Academy
Indiana Department of Education
Indianapolis, IN

Debra Lecklider
Assistant Professor, Director
The Experimental Program for Preparing School Principals
Butler University
Indianapolis, IN

Terry Russell
Principal
North Montgomery High School
Crawfordsville, IN

Gina Segobiano
Superintendent/Principal
Signal Hill School District 181
Belleville, IL

James Thompson, NCARB
President
Gibraltar Design, Inc.
Indianapolis, IN

Rene Townsend
Author, Executive Director
Public School Services
La Jolla, CA

Dana Trevethan
Principal
Turlock High School
Turlock, CA

Joyce Uglow
Principal
Lyons Center School
Burlington, WI

About the Authors

Robert E. Brower is superintendent for the North Montgomery Community School Corporation in Crawfordsville, Indiana. Besides these duties, Dr. Brower is a consultant and presenter for many educational issues. Some of these include trimester scheduling, discipline in schools, teaching on the extended period, leadership topics, decision-making philosophy, building professional staff capacity, and teaching for learning. Dr. Brower has also published articles in numerous professional journals on these topics. Dr. Brower is recognized nationally as an expert on trimester scheduling for both middle schools and high schools. He and Dr. Brad Balch invented the Transformational Leadership theory presented in this book. Dr. Brower is an entertaining presenter who mixes research with common sense. Dr. Brower's educational career has included teaching and coaching for 22 years, 6 years as a high school principal, and 4 years as a public school superintendent. This is Dr. Brower's first book, but several more are in the works.

Bradley V. Balch is currently the Chairperson for the Department of Educational Leadership, Administration, and Foundations at Indiana State University in Terre Haute, Indiana. Formerly, Dr. Balch served as a teacher, building administrator, and superintendent. In addition to his current capacity as a school board president, Dr. Balch also serves as a facilitator and consultant to school boards on leadership and governance issues. His scholarship agenda—including presentations and publications at the regional, state, and national levels—focuses in part on the recruitment, retention, and professional development of school leaders, mentoring and induction of new school leaders, and stress factors in district-level leadership.

1

Introduction

We are what we continually do.

—Aristotle

I t is 11:00 p.m., and as he drives home from a 15-hour work day at the office, the restful evening that Aaron Milner was hoping for with his family has eluded him once again. Aaron Milner is the superintendent of a large school district. As Aaron drives home from work, he is distracted by the impending events of the next day, knowing that what lies ahead is a daunting task; a dreaded decision that was inevitable and must be acted upon.

Aaron has wrestled and anguished over a decision to terminate the contract of a building principal, Roberta Zelling. Roberta has been a secondary school administrator in the district for 4 years and has entrenched herself as a powerful leader . . . one who is both loathed and loved depending on with whom one talks. She has been known to criticize Aaron publicly, make negative comments about other district administrators when talking with school board members, and make disparaging remarks about Aaron to her faculty and staff. During her employment tenure, Roberta has built effective, robust rapport with many school stakeholders; however, Aaron has had to have frequent meetings with Roberta and even tendered written reprimands noting her lack of tact, work ethic, inability to meet time lines, and questionable ethical practices in performing her job. Roberta has not responded to the constructive criticism appropriately. Instead of taking steps to improve, Roberta has endeavored to strengthen her position with others by undermining Aaron's authority in nearly every aspect of schooling. She has solidified herself as a powerful force within the culture of the school and district since her last unflattering formal evaluation. Aaron laments the fact that he inherited this personnel problem from the previous superintendent, whom he replaced 10 months earlier.

As Aaron eases his car down the road home, he is once again reminded that it is "lonely at the top." His angst makes it hard to find a comfortable driving position, and he longs to be in the comfort of his home. It is December 10th, and a light snow is falling outside. As Aaron nears his home, he can see a young rabbit hop aimlessly across the soft white snow that has gently covered the ground. The streetlight illuminates the shadow more than the creature as the young rabbit disappears into the dark. Aaron looks beyond the nearness to see all the houses lining the pristine landscape of his suburban neighborhood . . . only hints of light from the homes can be seen. He wonders what stress-filled events will befall his neighbors on the beckoning new day. Surely no one will be faced with such a daunting decision as he must make! Aaron's becomes distracted from his driving as he looks inward, almost hypnotically, to once again rehearse his mentally scripted meeting with his building administrator. Will she fight the termination? Will she label him a misogynist? Will she counterattack with charges directed at him? Will she appeal to board members with unfounded stories? Will she invent harassment or discrimination scenarios that would ruin his career? What would his wife think if trumped-up stories were revealed publicly? How will this termination affect other district schools, school employees, the 1,200 students she serves, and other administrators? Aaron's neck stiffens as he looks beyond the car to refocus on his driving. At the same time, the light snow settles on his windshield, momentarily disrupting his thoughts. As he reaches his driveway, Aaron realizes the restful evening he had craved was now hopelessly lost. He quietly eases from his car, straightening and stretching his ailing lower back; a reminder of the operation he had endured just 3 months earlier. He now understands why the doctor said that most back pain could be traced to stress. His anxiety level rises as the thought crosses his mind that he will most likely not sleep tonight. He thinks maybe he could call his family doctor to prescribe sleeping pills. Turning toward the house, and with a deep breath, Aaron slips through the front door to salvage his evening with his family, still distracted by the looming questions that plague his mind.

This scene, or similar anxiety-ridden scenes, permeate the very soul of school leaders at some time in their leadership careers. The names of the leaders are different, the educational institutions they lead are different, and even the types of decision making are different, but the angst that exists with all tough decisions rarely lifts. Difficult decisions compel school leaders, regardless of level or responsibility, to find solutions to minimize the anguish that surrounds complex and difficult decision making. Simply stated, the contemporary leader must act decisively and with conviction, knowing that every decision is made for the "right" reasons. A sound pedagogy of decision making helps to ensure that America's schools thrive. When educational institutions flourish, the people who comprise these institutions will flourish too. Often, the journey of ensuring institutional fulfillment can begin only after a leader's pedagogical shift.

As schools, families, governmental units, and other for-profit and not-for-profit institutions come of age in the new millennium, the struggle for school leaders to make good, productive decisions seems to have become clouded with ever-growing uncertainty and skepticism. In an era of high expectations for accountability and entitlement among school stakeholders, decisions can quickly backfire and blow up in the face of school leaders with profound adverse effects. At every juncture of decision making, it appears that school leaders are being criticized for their decisions by any one of a number of individuals or institutions, including their own employees. School leaders are also subject to media criticisms for decisions made that affect people, programs, and school facilities. These criticisms and the negative environment they create can overwhelm a leader, adversely affecting current and future decision making. Yielding to criticism and negative feedback can also create untenable situations that could cost a leader his or her position, creating professional and personal duress. Many good decisions can be overshadowed suddenly by one decision that adversely affects an individual or group of individuals. Enormous pressures are being placed on our nation's school leaders at the building and district level. These pressures are compounded when school leaders lack a sound decision-making pedagogy and attempt to be *all* things to *all* people.

Contemporary school leaders are expected to perform better than ever before, being held accountable for teaching and learning while constantly striving for improvement and serving as positive change agents. Additionally, these contemporary school leaders must foster a healthy and positive educational climate. It often seems impossible!

The challenges facing school leaders in a new millennium of decision making will require a well-articulated pedagogy—a transformational approach that allows for difficult decisions to be made. Many contemporary leaders already embrace a successful paradigm of thought—a transforming focus from what is good for the individual to one that reflects what is best for the common good. Simply stated, *transformational decision making* means thinking and acting in ways that reflect the common good as the leadership imperative, not the individual good.

Transformational decision making offers a sound, fundamental framework of pedagogy for all school leaders to effectively meet the challenges of contemporary thinking, acting, and decision making. It is an effective means of looking at complex institutions while giving leaders of these entities methods and strategies to tackle tough decisions with a clear conscience and thorough understanding. Conceptualizing this contemporary paradigm is to be at peace with decision making. Transformational decision making by the school leader will translate into healthy, successful, and effective institutions—the mission of transformational decision making.

In order to understand how school leaders often arrive at a confounding condition of anxiety-ridden thinking and decision making, past leadership practices must be examined, current priorities assessed, and a determination of future direction codified. In other words, can you clearly articulate your leadership and decision-making pedagogy? If not, take time to self-assess. The Resource contains a Decision Making Self-Assessment. Completing this assessment before reading further will give you an informed perspective with which to view the book's content. Self-honesty and a robust awareness of your own leadership and decision-making pedagogy are critical to effectiveness. Numerous educational leadership books have been published expounding on the virtues of great leadership, providing a framework with which to view leadership. Successful authors on the subject of leadership such as Ken Blanchard, Steven Covey, Edward Deming, Peter Drucker, John Gardner, Doug McGregor, Tom Peters, Peter Senge, and Thomas Sergiovanni, to name a few, have all contributed greatly to the body of recent scholarship on sound educational leadership. Yet transformational decision making focuses on a crucial characteristic of leadership that is tantamount to effective schooling and often overlooked. A significant void exists regarding sound, fundamental decision making for contemporary school leaders. One fact is certain amidst tremendous leadership; one bad or ill-conceived decision can eliminate or usurp an otherwise effective leader, lacking in great decision-making skills and absent an articulate conception of decision making. A sound understanding of transformational decision making is intended to complement the body of knowledge on leadership that currently exists and expand the knowledge base of school leadership in new and creative ways. Even great leaders struggle with tough decisions. Transformational decision making is intended to give leaders the knowledge necessary to make consistently effective decisions.

Although decisions in any school-based institution are intended to benefit the stakeholders, these same stakeholders make decision making challenging or difficult at times. Our judgments about decision making have been clouded by our concerns about ourselves, or how these decisions will affect people as individuals. A sound understanding of the "me" complex is necessary before grasping the understanding behind a decision-making paradigm shift.

Just a few decades ago, values-based priorities were profoundly different from today. Undeniably, our individual priorities regarding faith, country, family, self, and education have changed significantly in the past several decades. A philosophical shift in priorities often places the individual (i.e., self) first, creating fertile ground for ever-growing leadership challenges. It is critically important to understand this shifting phenomenon of priorities in order to accurately assess how they negatively influence decision making. Some leaders focus on how some action or decision will affect them or someone very close to them. This leads to determining whether to vote for it or against it, lobby for it or against it, argue for it or reject it, fight for it or run from it. The contemporary world remains largely about "me." Wrong or right, the basis of much decision making has a decades-old legacy of being rooted in how that decision will affect "me" or those near "me" (Prior, 2003; Wexler, 2003).

No doubt America's access to television and other emergent technologies has contributed to this societal shift in priorities from collective good to individual good by intensifying the instant and self-gratification of the information consumer. Information providers are continually competing to provide the "scoop," "eyewitness account," or "reality" version of almost anything perceived to be of interest. With this constant effort to "feed" information consumers, social values have been immersed in an orientation focused on the individual and his or her entitlement. The often shocking and provoking nature of information results in information consumers internalizing and personalizing these events. The anxiety-producing and instantaneous nature of information has the effect of creating a society whose values act to spin a protective cocoon around its individuals to keep one from harm's way. No doubt information systems (e.g., television, radio, Internet) have affected our actions, belief systems, and priorities more now than at any other time in our history. Similarly, school stakeholders have developed an expectation for well-embedded information systems that "feed" their instantaneous want of knowledge and information. These same stakeholders often want this information personalized (i.e., what does this mean for me), having the effect of inviting them into the decision-making loop.

America has also grown in recent years to become a nation of consumers. Although information continues to feed this desire, products and services in the not-for-profit sector have become an immense consumer target as well. America's obsession with "things" has had a profound influence on schools. A values shift in recent decades has led school stakeholders to approach schools from a consumer's perspective, expecting choice, shared decision making, and entitlement while advocating for individual and often selfish outcomes.

These phenomena, along with other societal changes, such as an eroding middle class, have affected priority shifts from the common good to the individual good. These shifts ultimately influence how school leaders make effective decisions for the institutions they lead. School stakeholders usually place themselves, their children, and their loved ones as the highest priority in decision making. To do otherwise is the exception and not the norm. This often creates havoc for effective decision making. Our love of self, our love of those closest to us, and our desire for personal contentment all detract from effective decision making.

A priority consideration for transformational leadership is, "What is in the best interest of our students, faculty, staff, board members, administrators, parents, taxpayers, etc?" School leaders make decisions based on what is in the best interest of people. This seems natural as one initially ponders decision making, because school leaders have been groomed to do, think, and decide in this way. Furthermore, people want to live happy and productive lives. It cannot be disputed that people are very important, but no individual is as important as the populations of people who form the collective good.

A fundamental pedagogy is embedded in the words *institution* and *transformational*. Institution is the name of various school entities, including, but not limited to, a school corporation, school, organization, team, department, classroom, or union. To be considered an institution, the entity must be composed of stakeholders (i.e., a membership) and have a purpose. Furthermore, an institution must have some type of formal or informal leadership (e.g., board president, superintendent, principal, teacher, coach, department chair, or spokesperson). An institution is intended to represent the common good of its stakeholders. Transformational decision making is a pedagogy based on what is in the best interest of the institution (i.e., the common good) rather than what is in the best interest of the individuals within the institution. As paradoxical and competing as it may seem, this is the essence of effective leadership decision making. Those embracing this pedagogy will fully understand why and how decisions are made, minimizing lengthy apologies or stress-laden responses immersed in a "me" orientation.

Summary

Most school leaders make great decisions some of the time, but few leaders make great decisions all of the time. The formula for great decision making can be understood and enjoyed if transformational decision making is embraced in an institutional context. Transformational decision making means thinking and acting in ways that reflect the common good of an educational institution. Broadly defined, institutions include any school entity that is composed of a membership (i.e., any school stakeholders), has a purpose, and possesses some type of formal or informal leadership.

Why do school leaders sometimes find it difficult to act decisively and effectively? What are the essential concepts for decision making, and how and why should school leaders act with a clear conscience in difficult decision-making situations? A rich base of scholarship exists regarding educational leadership, yet none of these renderings have sought the heart of decision-making pedagogy for contemporary leaders to answer these challenging questions in a way that is easy to understand and universally applicable.

Reflective Thinking

1. Imagine the most difficult decision you have made. Which aspects of the decision-making process went well? Which aspects of the decision-making process were challenges?

2. When you make a difficult decision, how do you respond to criticism and negative feedback?

3. What did you learn about yourself from the Decision Making Self-Assessment in the Resource?

2

Decision-Making Pedagogy

A Leadership Essential

Example is leadership.

—Albert Schweitzer

It was mid-March, and Molly Hampton had just arrived at work. In her role as Director of Curriculum for a metropolitan school district, Molly arrived in her office at precisely 6:45 a.m., just like every other day. There was a light drizzle of rain coming straight down from the black sky, but Molly always left her house according to the weather conditions, because her office arrival at the same time each day was important to her. Some employees in Molly's office even called her "high strung" because of her "Type A" personality. Molly took off her jacket and leaned forward to turn on her computer when a slight pain shot down her upper back and through her arm . . . a quick reminder of the stress she was feeling the past couple of weeks. As she waited for the computer to boot and allow her to log on, Molly sat reflectively at her desk peering outside into the nothingness of the morning. Molly and a committee in her charge had to make some very difficult decisions that affected every teacher and student in the school district, and she anticipated that these decisions would upset some district stakeholders. Molly felt that the anger would be directed largely at her. Molly clicked on the coffee pot beside her desk and calmness began to engulf her as she prepared to face the morning when the final decisions would be codified.

Molly was undergoing a transformation of thinking since the school board administrative team completed a work session 2 months earlier, outlining a new leadership pedagogy to help with making difficult decisions. During Molly's 30-minute drives to and from work since the decision-making work session, she spent countless hours making meaning of the guidelines that frame this new pedagogy of leadership decision making. It all seemed so easy to her at the work session, but her looming committee meeting later in the morning would be the real test for Molly.

Molly's superintendent and school board had much confidence in her leadership, entrusting Molly to make the final decision on three major reform issues that had been under consideration for more than a year. The leadership of the district was solidly behind these efforts of reform. In fact, a mandate for change had been approved by the board, challenging the district to restructure much of how instruction is delivered and evaluated. The following was a list of decisions that were finally approved by the board amid union opposition. Meaningful discussion with the teachers' union had occurred, but they would not give final approval for the reforms that had implications for change in their working conditions.

1. A new teacher evaluation instrument reflecting standards-based teaching will take effect the following school year.

2. A new grade card for students that reflected the state standards and an indication of mastery of these standards will be used in conjunction with grades, beginning the following year.

3. Students on a diploma track at the high school must demonstrate mastery of the state standards and pass the state graduation exam in order to earn a diploma.

Molly convened a committee whose charge was addressing the directives. The committee was composed of four teachers, each representing the buildings in the district, an elementary and secondary principal, a school board member, three parents, two members of the local chamber of commerce, and herself. Molly's tenth and final meeting was scheduled for this morning at 7:30 a.m. in the boardroom.

When the committee first met many months ago, Molly was not aware of the new transformational decision-making pedagogy that was introduced to her a few months earlier. She was not in a position to share this new pedagogy with committee members in the beginning. This lack of framework would often haunt Molly as the committee worked through many difficult issues. This final three meetings were Molly's first interactions with the committee since learning about transformational decision making. Because Molly did not previously have a consistent framework to make decisions, there were times when destructive organizational dynamics influenced the committee. Often, selfish (i.e., me first) opinions and assumptions permeated the discussion. Facts and evidence were considered but largely overlooked because of the implications for change. Instead, facts and evidence were disaggregated in ways that supported the status quo and strengthened resistance to the board's directives. Even Molly was guilty of limiting the work of the committee. Molly had strong feelings as to what the committee's outcomes should be. Over time, her feelings became known to the group, thwarting diverse opinion and meaningful consensus. Except for the final three meetings, what consensus did emerge felt contrived, as if committee members were saying, "You've told us what the outcomes will be, so let's get this charade over with."

But things were different now. . . . Molly's confidence level rose with each day since the leadership decision making inservice. The more she reflected on the transformational pedagogy, the more Molly knew that the work of the committee was beginning to model a sound framework for decision making. Molly's strategy for the final three meetings, which included three critical constructs of decision making, were as follows: First, provide a quick overview of how the decisions were going to be made using portions of the transformational decision-making framework that aligned with her leadership and current situation. This included reviewing the board directives in terms of the district's vision and mission to ensure that the decisions would be aligned with these distinct identities (i.e., the vision and mission); facilitating dialogue that focused on the common good to minimize discussion at the individual (i.e., me first) stakeholder level; improving respect and rapport by inviting all perspectives and openly discussing everyone's roles and responsibilities as a committee member; and communicating a message of entrustment by truly valuing members and affirming their role in a leadership capacity. Second, Molly would make it clear that decisions should be largely influenced by facts, objective data, and other forms of evidence. Third, Molly would explain the difficulty of these ultimate decisions and the predictable nature of the criticism that would follow. Her explanations were immersed in conceptions of change and suggestions for building greater change capacity in the district.

The final meeting lasted approximately 3 hours. Much dialogue occurred, and conflict did arise; however, the previous respect and rapport-building opportunities kept conflict at a professional, not personal, level. As the difficult decisions were codified, consensus emerged more easily because of the evidence-based focus, alignment with the vision and mission, and common good (i.e., students in this case) orientation.

This real-life example illustrates three important points. First, without a consistent decision-making pedagogy, consensus does not develop around difficult decisions. Rather, a single individual is often left to own the decision with little stakeholder buy-in. Second, difficult decisions usually result in change, giving rise to conflict. Understanding change and building capacity for change minimizes the impact of difficult decisions. Finally, decision making is situational and leadership specific. A one-size-fits-all pedagogy will not work. Educational leaders must understand their own identity and craft a decision-making pedagogy based on this understanding. Decisions will also be made in a variety of situations (e.g., school boards, negotiations, committees, team meetings) drawing on different dimensions of a decision-making pedagogy.

Through years of empirical observation, a growing body of scholarship—as well as practices related to school leadership, a theory of decision making, and the effects this has on leadership—has developed. The pedagogy used to describe this theory is transformational decision making. The concept is merely an articulation of ideas that some leaders already use on a daily basis. For many leaders, transformational decision making will confirm their current pedagogical practice, offering contemporary leaders peace of mind as they continue their leadership journey. Whether the reader is embracing new decision-making theories to enhance leadership practices or affirming current leadership pedagogies, transformational concepts will meet with the greatest success when leaders raise awareness among other school stakeholders about transformational decision making. As with all change, it must become part of a school or district's culture and permeate the daily climate in order to have a significant and meaningful impact. In fact, all school stakeholders, not just school leaders, can reap tremendous benefit from the pedagogical shift of transformational decision making.

Transformational decision making is manifested in a variety of institutional settings. Institutions may include school corporations, schools, organizations, teams, departments, classrooms, or unions. They must be composed of stakeholders (i.e., a membership), have a purpose, have a type of formal or informal leadership, and represent the common good of their stakeholders. Various institutional examples are illustrated in Figure 2.1. Although not all-inclusive, Figure 2.1 depicts an unusual "upside-down wedding cake" of institutions when viewed through the lens of decision making—an inexorable tie bound by membership, purpose, and the common good with implications that the decisions of larger institutions may have precedence over the decisions of smaller institutions.

Institutions do not always have a physical identity, but rather exist in context. For example, one can easily visualize a school, but a

Figure 2.1   Representative Institutions Affecting Transformational
Decision Making

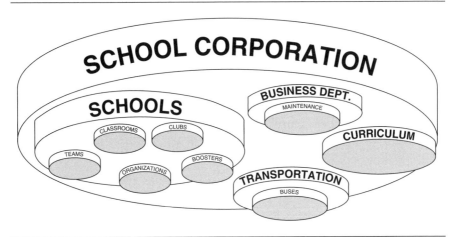

team exists in context. Institutions can remain unchanged or can be reconfigured and redesigned. Institutions can be stable or can be in constant flux, because they are composed of people (i.e., stakeholders), and people can come and go in any institution. Institutions can keep the same name for years or may change their names based on consolidation or newly created institutions. Leaders can change, but the institution remains. New institutions are formed every day, and some can even disappear as quickly. Yet institutions cannot be described with normal adjective labels that are used commonly to describe people, objects, or places.

Educational centers are institutions. These include universities, colleges, high schools, middle schools, elementary schools, service centers, athletic teams, clubs, classrooms, and parent-teacher organizations. Profit-seeking and production- or service-oriented centers are institutions, too. These include businesses, companies, partnerships, or corporations. Governmental units are also institutions. These include countries, counties, states, cities, divisions, and councils. Community clubs and organizations are considered institutions. These include service clubs, fraternities, sororities, scouting groups, professional organizations, and philosophical clubs. Religious groups, militaries, musical groups, and thousands of others are all considered institutions. Although not all-inclusive, the preceding list exemplifies the breadth of institutions' landscape. However, educational leadership and the institutions it serves will be the focus of this book.

Institutions can stand alone or be embedded within other institutions. An example of this interdependence would be a state department for education, a school corporation, a school within the school corporation, and a classroom/team/club within the particular school. The same could be illustrated for businesses, corporations, factories, large organizations, governmental units, or the military. If one uses the umbrella or upside-down wedding cake metaphors, the umbrella or largest tier of the wedding cake is the overriding institution, and there can be hundreds of interdependent institutions under the umbrella or largest tier of the wedding cake. All are individual entities and require decision making for the particular institutions; yet institutional interdependence permeates the structure and bonds it together.

Institutions have formal and informal leaders. There are leaders of thousands of institutions, having a variety of titles. Some of these leadership names include parent, custodian, teacher, principal, superintendent, governor, school board president, treasurer, secretary, and so on.

As mentioned earlier, members of an institution can change; the place where members meet can change; the buildings that house the members can change; the structure can change; the complexion can change; and the name can change. However, despite the many avenues of change that institutions can undertake, the *context* of a particular institution never changes. In other words, amid change, the context of the institution will remain, even while taking on a new institutional form. Other institutions will merge and form new institutions. For example, in any particular school district, teachers and students are constantly changing, and buildings are replaced, renovated, or raised, but the institution of a particular school remains the same. Sometimes, a school will be raised or abandoned and may be replaced with a newly named building, but the institution will continue to exist, just in a new location. At times, particular institutions are closed, destroyed, and not re-formed. In those cases, that specific institution may no longer exist and decision making ceases. Obviously, at that point, no decision making is warranted for the extinct institution, but decision making about structures of the extinct institution may be shifted to another institution. An example of this is building closure.

There are millions of institutions around us. Some are created daily, and others are centuries old. Remember, an institution must include stakeholders, it must have a defined purpose or cause, and it must have some type of formal or informal leadership in place.

To further elucidate when an institution exists, consider three friends going to the mall or meeting in the morning for coffee. These groups are not institutions by definition. If these same people meet on a regular basis for the purpose of buying stocks and share formal or informal leadership, then it becomes an institution. Leadership can and should be shared between several people. Leadership has to be present in some form to meet the definition of an institution. An administrator who empowers a teacher in the school for a leadership task is an example of shared leadership and an institutional dynamic.

Transformational decision making, thinking, and acting in ways that reflect the common good rather than the individual good involve leaders and members of an institution embracing a common pedagogy immersed in Transformational Laws. The following is a list of pedagogical constructs called laws that guide decision making:

1. Leaders understand and practice a consistent decision-making pedagogy.

2. Leaders are aware of the internal obstacles to decision making.

3. Leaders recognize the external barriers to decision making.

4. Leaders align decision-making practices with their mission.

5. Leaders know the fundamental laws of human nature.

6. Leaders define relationships with rapport and respect.

7. Leaders appreciate the value of empowerment and delegation.

8. Leaders value meaningful motivation.

9. Leaders understand capitalism and its competitive influences.

10. Leaders comprehend educational change.

11. Leaders recognize the destructive pitfalls in decision making.

12. Leaders promote a consistent decision-making pedagogy among all stakeholders.

The clear mandate of the school leader is to make decisions based on what is in the best interest of the institution. At times, transformational decision making is in conflict with what is in the best interest of certain individuals. Herein lies the importance of effective decision making. Too often, leaders have angst over what is in the best interest of particular individuals in the institution. This is a persistent pitfall of sound decision making. This self-imposed stressor damages a leader's ability to make great decisions for the institution he or she leads. No doubt some decisions will not meet with the approval of some individuals or groups of individuals, but the goal of a leader is to lead the institution in positive and effective ways with a strong sense of vision and purpose for the common good.

If the leader of a given school district decides that several jobs must be eliminated to ensure the district's survival, then the leader can make this difficult decision with a clear conscience when transformational decision making is used for the common good. Difficult decisions that involve people's livelihood are often central to the long-term health of a school or district and cannot be avoided. To a casual observer or a stakeholder directly or indirectly affected by a personnel decision, it may appear to be misdirected and simply wrong. However, for the leader who acts with transformational decision making, the decision is not only right, but also most likely the only decision worthy of a good outcome in the long run.

A typical example of challenging transformational decision making might be a student who is expelled from high school because he or she dealt drugs on school property. The school administration determined that the expulsion of this student will help the institution maintain the safety and well-being of the entire student population (i.e., the common good) and their right to an education. Armed with this pedagogical belief, the expulsion of the student can be deemed in the best interest of the institution. The student, the student's parents, and even some teachers may disagree with the expulsion on personal grounds, but the common good provided the decision-making rationale. Those not agreeing with the decision will most likely argue that the severity of an expulsion is potentially harmful by denying the student his or her right to an education. When one examines transformational thinking in this regard, the question can no longer be what is in the best interest of the student, but rather what is in the best interest of the institution. If the administrators felt that the danger to the school institution was greater by allowing the expelled student back into the school, then they made a transformational decision and it was absolutely the right decision. School administrators or leaders in general will be faced with these tough decisions almost daily, but if these leaders always act in transformationally sound ways, the decisions can be made easily, consistently, and without regret. Ultimately, everyone benefits by leading transformationally.

If the coach of an athletic team (i.e., an athletic institution) must cut a high-ability player to maintain positive team chemistry, the coach can make this tough decision knowing it is in the best interest of the team. Effective coaches know that what is best for the team may not always be what is best for an individual on the team. If a player tries to make a conference all-star team by shooting excessively and to the detriment of team success, then the team suffers as a result of these actions. This challenges sound institutional culture, and the leader must act to correct this potentially fatal problem. By emphasizing team goals rather than individual player gains, the leader is acting in transformational ways. The potential all-star, his or her family, and even certain community members may disagree with the coach's decision to redirect the player's gifts and talents into the team concept, but the individual is not the concern . . . only the institution. Interestingly enough, if the coach embraces a transformational decision-making pedagogy, the player is more likely to make the all-star team and will most likely learn an important life lesson about sacrificing individual gain for the common good.

In these examples, individuals or those close to them are directly affected by the decisions of their leaders. Yet the important and determining factor in decision making is not the individual in these decisions, but rather the institution to which they belong. As difficult as this pedagogy is for some people to accept, it is essential to effective transformational decision making. When leaders make decisions based on what is good for the institution, guided by respect and dignity for the individuals that comprise the institution, they become transformational thinkers. The institutions they lead will flourish as a result.

Summary

Because decision making is complex, not all decisions made by school leaders will be correct. However, informed leaders of this pedagogy can be assured that if they fully understand the Transformational Laws shared in the following chapters, their leadership will be more effective, consistent, and better understood by those affected as a result of the decisions. Furthermore, the Transformational Laws of decision making must be articulated and embedded in all interdependent institutions and shared with individuals in each institution to truly affect climate and culture in meaningful ways. It gives leaders the satisfaction of having a foundation of pedagogical leadership for decision making that makes their jobs more effective and tenable, while allowing school stakeholders the opportunity to understand and practice transformational decision making as well. No doubt disagreement and conflict will occur, but climates and cultures underscored by transformational decision making will survive short-term obstacles, creating improved capacities for teaching and learning to prosper.

Conceptual Framework

1. Define the institutions that exist in your educational setting. Consider the decision-making leadership you provide for these institutions. What other types of formal or informal leadership exist within these institutions that affect your decision making?

2. Apply the upside-down wedding cake to your institutions. Define the interdependence that exists above and below the institutions for which you provide leadership. Do the interdependent institutions have aligned missions, visions, and goals? If not, interdependence may be contrived and conflict-laden.

Reflective Thinking

1. Institutions may be visualized as an upside-down wedding cake when viewed through the lens of decision making. What other ways could an educational institution be visualized, and why?

2. Describe a decision you made that was in conflict with certain individuals, yet benefited the common good. Did the decision cause you angst and serve as a source of stress? How did you deal with the conflict?

3. Is your decision making consistent and predictable for the institution you serve? Are easy, day-to-day decisions handled consistently? Are difficult, divisive decisions handled consistently?

3

Overcoming Internal Obstacles to Decision Making

*It is what we do when no one is
looking that truly defines character.*

—Andrew Carnegie

Numerous obstacles can cloud positive and fundamental deci-sion making. It is commonly understood that effective leaders make conscious decisions. However, leaders are distinct in the ways they gather information and make decisions based on information. Although the means of gathering this information are diverse, effec-tive leaders nevertheless make conscious decisions based on gathering and considering multiple sources of information. Far less frequently, decisions are instinctive or safety/survival reactions to events.

Decisions are often based on some type of need. Philosophies of human needs vary. For example, Glasser (1986) notes five human needs: survival, love, freedom, fun, and control. Additional needs might be safety, belonging, and meaning. According to Maslow

(1954), there is a hierarchy of human needs that is arranged in ways that affect our behavior. These include physiological needs, security needs, social needs, recognition needs, and self-actualization needs. Regardless of the philosophy of human needs embraced, under-standing and acknowledging the fundamental needs that drive a per-son's personal and professional life are essential to making sound decisions from a leadership perspective.

Simply stated, human needs can manifest themselves as obstacles to transformational decision making. Understanding the contexts in which these needs manifest themselves as obstacles in daily human decision making and the internal and external pressures that these needs exert on leadership is essential. Understanding human nature and people's needs helps leaders to understand the individual dynamic as it relates to the common good and the institution.

The following list describes common obstacles that can create problems in decision making. Understanding and acknowledging this list can help transformational school leaders see themselves objectively and strengthen decision-making capacity by creating the clear conscience needed to be an effective and thriving leader. The obstacles to transformational decision making include the following:

1. The leader makes immoral, unethical, or illegal decisions.

2. The leader has a serious addiction that clouds great decision making.

3. The leader forms bad habits of character or personality.

4. The leader allows the "what's best for me or someone close to me" syndrome to hinder effective decision making.

5. The leader lets distracting influences affect decision making.

6. The leader's "heart" can overpower sound decision making.

7. The leader lacks the professional disposition to explain tough decisions and encourage buy-in.

8. The leader fears implementation fallout from decisions.

9. The leader lacks a clear institutional vision or mission.

10. The leader lacks the resolve to tackle tough decisions.

These 10 obstacles are not intended to be all-inclusive but rather are offered as core examples of obstacles that persistently taint decision making.

The leader makes immoral, unethical, or illegal decisions. It is impossible for a leader to make good decisions if he or she is not trustworthy. Covey (1990) notes that being trustworthy on a personal level is a fundamental principle of great leadership. Without being trustworthy on a personal level, one is not free to give trust on an interpersonal level. Making unethical, immoral, or illegal decisions are practices that quickly erode trustworthiness and will eventually lead to the downfall of the leader. Often, during an untrustworthy leader's tenure, numerous decisions are made that spell doom for the leader because the decisions are questioned on moral, ethical, or legal grounds. Sadly, numerous noteworthy leaders in history have violated fundamental rules of moral, ethical, and legal governance, scripting their eventual doom. Suffice it to say that violating stakeholder trust is tantamount to disaster in leadership decision making. It is often best stated in the adage "a clear conscience is the softest pillow." Acting in moral, ethical, and legal ways 100% of the time makes decision making much easier, is far less complicated, and builds trust. It is the only way!

The leader has a serious addiction that clouds great decision making. Nearly everyone has some form of addiction, whether healthy or unhealthy. Healthy addictions might include comfort foods, caffeine, or exercise. Unhealthy addictions might include alcohol, drugs, or gambling. When the addiction is so pervasive that it can negatively influence sound decision making, it becomes a detriment to the leader. Addictions are easily disguised and hard to reveal, and they can remain unnoticed by those closest to the person with the addiction. Addiction complicates the entire process of leadership, which ultimately can result in flawed decision making by eroding the focus on the common good and supplanting it with the need to satisfy an addiction. Addictions that have created havoc with decision making include gambling, drugs, alcohol, money, power, and illicit Internet use. Addictions can taint the decision-making process by introducing obstacles of selfishness and gratification that simply muddy the waters of clear decision making. Addictions or disease affect many institutional stakeholders. Sound leadership requires an understanding of the obstacles that addictions and disease can create when striving to make great decisions and an acknowledgment of which addictions could potentially affect one's own decision making.

The leader forms bad habits of character or personality. Shortcomings of human character can often result in less-than-effective leadership and decision making by compromising the essential focus on the common good. Bad habits that are character related might include lying, cheating, dishonesty, evasiveness, sarcasm, threats, intimidation, and lack of work ethic. And although adversity in the educational setting often builds or destroys leadership character, it also *reveals* character in leadership practice. It often takes a significant traumatic event or genuine desire for change in basic character to occur—yet change can occur. If a leader exhibits poor habits of character, failed decision making will ultimately follow. Personality traits such as arrogance, overconfidence, intimidation, fear, lack of fear, and piousness affect decision making in ways that negatively affect institutions by detracting from the common good. These personality traits might serve other leaders, but for the contemporary school leader, there is rarely an instance when these traits are effective for institutions. At times, some of these could be construed as assets and not liabilities, but a continued propensity to exhibit these personality traits will eventually have an adverse effect on effective decision-making abilities.

The leader allows the "what's best for me or someone close to me" syndrome to hinder effective decision making. There is abundant evidence to suggest our country has developed a "me first" attitude toward decision making. Anything that is valued as good or bad in a "me first" culture is largely determined on an individual basis, depending on how it will affect the individual or someone close to the individual. Many school stakeholders have a difficult time seeing the big picture or the larger institutional landscape. Too many stakeholders of education have adopted a micro, not macro, viewpoint. The adage of seeing the trees, but failing to see the forest, best describes this notion. Whether one agrees or disagrees with a particular decision is largely dependent upon how it will affect "me" or someone close to "me." The leader of any institution must exercise vigilance to make decisions based on what is in the best interest of the institution and not what may be in the best interest of the leader or someone close to the leader. This can be a significant obstacle in decision making. Great leadership and decision making must never let the "me first" syndrome affect decisions. Relinquishing ourselves to this obstacle will ultimately destroy good institutional faith. Understanding and acknowledging this obstacle is a large step in implementing sound transformational decision making.

The U.S. Civil War can give the reader many examples of how this "me first" thinking was not a factor, but could have been a factor. Reflecting on Joshua Chamberlain's leadership in the battle of Little Round Top at Gettysburg in July 1863, he did not succumb to "me first" thinking. If he had capitulated to thinking about what was in his best personal interests at the time, he may very well have retreated from the Little Round Top after his troops expended their ammunition and were faced with total annihilation. Instead, and against all odds, Chamberlain ordered a bayonet charge that saved the Union flank against the Confederacy and all but assured victory for the North in the Battle of Gettysburg. Some military leaders facing similar circumstances might well have conceded defeat to save their own lives. Similar examples can be found today in education. On April 19, 1999, the Columbine High School tragedy shocked the world, and a fallen hero emerged, Mr. David Sanders. Mr. Sanders sacrificed his life with a total disregard for "me first" by placing students, colleagues, and the high school's institutional common good first, amid horrific acts of violence. Although Chamberlain's and Sanders's acts are heroic, similar acts of "me first" defiance can be found in the daily practice of teaching, learning, and leading.

The leader lets distracting influences affect decision making. Undue influence by people with connections, influential positions, money, property, or similar types of power can influence sound decision making. People who also exploit the "Law of Firsts" can also unduly influence leaders. Simply put, this means that leaders have a tendency to be influenced by the person or persons who share their perspectives "first." Transformational leaders understand the importance of gathering multiple perspectives and understanding the role of power in the decision-making process. If leaders are not careful, distracting influences can misguide objective thinking by aligning decision making with those who are the most persuasive, powerful, or "first." Distracting influences may have nothing to do with the institutional common good.

The famous poet Robert Frost was credited with saying, "There are only three things in the world: religion, science, and gossip." Similarly, it might be said that leaders make decisions from three perspectives: faith, fact, and opinion. Nearly all decisions are made with input compiled from innumerable sources. Even if a leader does not rely on external influences, decisions likely will be made from a basic, predictable framework that involves one or more sources, such as Frost's paradigm. These sources can be thought of as three distinct types of input: faith that something will work, objective fact that is scientifically founded or has a likelihood of success based on empirical evidence, and personal and professional opinion. When the decisions made by school leaders are observed, they are likely influenced by three broad categories: faith, fact, and opinion.

Faith of any kind is not bound by empirical data or evidence. When one bases his or her judgments on faith, little evidence can be offered that will sway a person from the power of faith. However, one can argue that there is empirical truth in many faith-based perspectives, and most leaders would acknowledge that they have relied on faith at one time or another as a basis for decision making. Faith here means nothing more than a belief that something is true based on a deeply held value or belief that rarely wavers. Furthermore, this faith is so strong and pervasive that nothing can change the person's views regardless of other perspectives. Faith as a basis of decision making will certainly be challenged in an era of educational accountability and standards immersion, based largely on outputs, not inputs such as faith. Additionally, faith is only a marginal way for leaders to ask, "What is working and what is not?"

Sometimes, leaders make decisions based on faith. Many times, these deeply held beliefs and values are so strong that they can contaminate transformational decision making in the form of bias or prejudice. For example, an elementary principal might believe that intermediate-age students should not be taught algebra concepts because they have not reached an academic maturity that is required. She supports this bias with the belief that repetition of facts and their attendant memorization is the first learning step, and algebra merely impedes the fact-based method of teaching and learning.

Leaders must make decisions based on empirical and statistically sound input and not merely on faith alone. Faith alone in decision-making input can diminish the leader's effectiveness and marginalize the institution he or she leads. Faith is much more personal and introspective. Transformational leadership is more externally driven and less internally motivated. Transformational thinking requires leaders to use external empirical data and less faith to make decisions. This removes the leader from the subjective arena of bias and prejudice, placing him or her in the objective domain where sound decision making resides.

The most destructive and potentially fatal input to decision making is that formed by opinion. It is human nature to have an opinion regarding decisions, especially those affected by the decision either directly or indirectly. Opinion should be considered subjective, personal, and internally motivated with often-selfish motives. All of these considerations are counterproductive to institutional thinking. Everyone has attended a meeting in any number of institutions that involved discussions about decisions to be made. These discussions are outstanding ways to build consensus. During these discussions, it invariably happens that someone will say, "In my opinion, I think. . . ." With the "me first" mentality so pervasive in our world today, these statements are rampant among educational stakeholders. People's opinions are weighted not so much on the merits of the actual opinion offered, but rather on who is offering the opinion and how (e.g., making an emotional plea). In other words, a strong and/or influential person giving input into any discussion can carry enormous weight with regard to the final decision. Acceptance of an opinion based on source has only limited merit and frequently stifles discussion or dialogue. Groups of people can also form alliances of opinion and thwart sound decision making. Transformational leaders should direct meeting participants to minimize opinion and adopt perspectives based on objective, empirical data. When a leader practices transformational leadership by educating meeting participants about the pitfalls of opinionated dialogue, input is more likely to be objective and, thus, sound. Transformational leaders must continually remind stakeholders who gather together to help with decision making that they are to provide input based on facts, not perceptions; data, not gossip; and evidence, not opinion.

A true story exists of the farmer who ignored the meteorologists and began planting his fields a week too early because it was his opinion that the experts have been wrong more times than not regarding late frosts in the Midwest. The meteorologists were calling for an extended cold spell that might damage early corn because of freezing conditions and frost. However, the weather had been warm, and the fields were ready for planting. The farmer decided to trust his instincts and opinion, and planted nearly one third of his corn crop. The farmer was convinced he was right and the experts were wrong once again. As a result, the farmer lost more than 500 acres of his corn crop because of frost when the freezing temperatures arrived, just as predicted. Even if the farmer had been right and the meteorologists wrong, the risk was based on opinion and not empirical data. The gamble to wait was one based on objective data, and the gamble to plant was based on subjective data. Too often, educators gamble in similar ways by teaching and leading from the heart, disregarding evidence that might dictate a very different teaching and learning practice. When educators lead only from the heart, they gamble with student outcomes and fail to ask the critical and objective question, "What is working and what is not?"

Too often, the first perspectives considered in decision making involve input based on faith and input based on opinion. Both are highly subjective and may lead to erroneous decision making. The only effective and rational way to use input is through transformational thinking. Transformational thinking requires that leaders use sound evidence—such as statistical data, objective input, and empirically proven methods—to make decisions and advance the common good. When one uses input data that are not biased with personal thoughts and opinions, the decision is more likely to be accepted and effective in the long run.

Transformational leadership requires a certain amount of flexibility when looking at input data and making decisions. However, transformational leaders must strive to use facts, hard data, empirical proof, objective criteria, and the scientific methods of evidence collection, whenever reasonably appropriate to do so, when making decisions. Transformational thinking requires leaders to look at situations in ways that remove the leader from the personal aspects of decision making. A consistent problem with decision making has been the subjective nature used to make decisions. The "me first" mentality has further eroded effective decision making. Using sound evidence ensures that a leader will make decisions based on input that is beyond personal bias. This is the foundation of transformational thinking.

The farmer who gambles with weather is a perfect example of how a leader of his own business made a bad decision that could very well bankrupt his operation, or at the very least create financial hardships. The meteorologists use objective, scientific, and empirical data to make projections based on evidence. Once the farmer succumbed to using his "gut feeling" or opinion, and ignoring expert evidence, he placed himself in a position that could not be justified using transformational thinking. Similarly, teachers and administrators as transformational leaders who operate primarily from the heart ignore objective, scientific, and empirical evidence that could inform and improve teaching and learning.

Contemporary leaders must resist discussions and input from individuals and groups that rely heavily on opinion and faith as criteria for decision making. An effective leader will immerse educational stakeholders in discussions of transformational thinking to avoid subjective notions in favor of objective evidence with the goal of delivering sound decisions. When educational stakeholders are aware of and practicing transformational decision making, the institution can thrive and prosper.

For a leader, it is essential to listen to all perspectives, compelling or otherwise, when gathering information prior to decision making. By remaining objective and not making initial statements of intent or direction, the effective leader can make the final decision with a clear conscience and with clear vision while taking into account all viewpoints from a collaborative-consensus perspective. Any influence in this process by subjective input will only add to the probability that a bad decision may follow. The contemporary leader understands the importance of staying objective during the information-gathering stage of decision making.

The leader's heart can overpower sound decision making. Great leaders are great listeners, too. They listen empathically and with their hearts, but empathic listening and caring must not drive the decision-making pedagogy of the leader. If leaders continually make decisions primarily from their hearts, it might feel good, but it may destroy the leaders and the institutions they lead when tough decisions fail to materialize in effective ways. Yet leaders should consider individual need, and empathize and do everything in their power to support outcomes that minimize the hardship of those being adversely affected by a decision. However, leaders must exhibit the tenacity and fortitude to make decisions in the best interest of the institution and not based on what their heart may tell them to do. In doing so, decisions become consistent and predictable—two essential qualities of the transformational leader. There are also times when a leader must be careful not to make decisions that are vindictive or spiteful. This can happen when ill feelings exist toward an individual or group. A leader can find it tempting to disparage individuals or groups who have seemingly been thorns in his or her side, but the effective leader should not allow this to influence the decision-making process. Leaders must practice leading with the brain, while remembering the importance of the heart in decision making.

The leader lacks the professional disposition to explain tough decisions and encourage buy-in. Little can take the place of experience and ongoing professional development when it comes to leadership and effective decision making. Yet there are instances when people have ascended to great leadership positions through experience and mere hard work. Leaders have also emerged through competence and expertise. Sometimes, leaders have been thrust into leadership roles beyond their choosing (e.g., nepotism or dire circumstances), but they have nevertheless survived to become effective. In each of these exceptions, these leaders have succeeded because they mustered essential dispositions for success. All leaders, regardless of how they assumed their leadership position, must have the skills required to explain and encourage buy-in of tough decisions. If the leader cannot explain his or her decisions effectively, the institution can stray from its intended purpose (i.e., the vision and mission), adversely affecting the institution's climate and culture. The leader is also the cheerleader, the public relations person, and the salesperson who delivers the goods and services of understanding and meaning to those affected by the decisions. Stakeholders may not agree with decisions, but they deserve an opportunity to share in the decision-making process and ultimately know why and how a decision was reached. A very sound decision can result in an obstacle to successful implementation when the leader fails to achieve meaningful buy-in of the decision that was made. Buy-in should not be confused with manipulation. Buy-in implies that the rules of transformational decision making are embraced in a way that solicits meaningful input from diverse populations of stakeholders prior to making a decision. Once a decision is made, it is communicated through one- and two-way venues with an explanation that is grounded in the common good and aligned with the institution's purpose (i.e., the vision and mission).

The leader fears implementation fallout from decisions. Decisions to external school stakeholders can, at times, seem simple because the picture of decision making seems so clear from a distance (i.e., not involved in the complexities of making the decisions). Many times, being on the inside can create a very different decision-making picture; one that is confounded by the quagmire of negativism or the power of status quo that frequently permeates educational decision making. A leader can fall prey to the fear that stalks nearly everyone once tough decisions are announced and the implementation of the decision commences. The fear of implementation fallout can paralyze the leader, causing inaction or improper action in an effort to minimize the impact of the difficult decision. A clear vision of direction is needed without fear taking a powerful grip on the leader. Great leaders exhibit little fear of implementation fallout. They act boldly and decisively without fear of reprisal or threat. Fear and hesitation will cripple even the best intentions. A great leader can confidently say, "This decision is in the best interest of teaching and learning, and it supports our vision and mission!" If the leader cannot make these bold claims, then it is better to let those who are resilient to implementation fallout make the crucial decisions. Implementation fallout commences when stakeholders have filtered and interpreted a leader's decision. The value-added "me first" filter to interpret decisions often gives rise to criticism or outright rejection of the decision. However, those who employ transformational leadership can live with their decisions and build capacities for implementation with confidence, knowing the institution's common good prevailed.

The leader lacks a clear institutional vision or mission. A shared, compelling vision and mission is a must for any school leader to exhibit. Without a good roadmap (i.e., the mission) to guide the leader toward the institutional dream (i.e., the vision), the educational trip will be infinitely more difficult. Chance and uncontrollable circumstances are inherent parts of any institution; when leaders depend on chance or circumstance to guide them, they risk failure and directional uncertainty. Every great leader moves institutional stakeholders toward an aligned vision with a sound mission and works hard to achieve buy-in regarding the institution's vision and mission. This is not an easy task for any leader to undertake. Nevertheless, the institutional vision and mission must be embedded from top to bottom. Once the vision is in place, the leader's resolve is to move the institution via the mission in positive ways that ensure the livelihood of the institution. Shared visioning and collaborative missioning are all noteworthy strategies to achieve cohesion and understanding in any institution, but ultimately, the leader is responsible for implementing the vision and mission, keeping stakeholders focused on the dream and the roadmap to achieve the dream. Although the vision changes and the mission may be in constant flux, the leader remains the champion of the vision and mission, and the school stakeholders become the gatekeepers.

The leader lacks the resolve to tackle tough decisions. Some leaders, although not exhibiting fear or worry about threats or other fallout from difficult decisions, may simply lack the resolve to tackle tough decisions. This can be attributable to many things, including personal concerns (e.g., "me first") or a situation where the leader just does not want to upset the status quo when things are seemingly okay. Why change when everything appears like it is running smoothly and efficiently? In other words, why fix what's not broken? Great leaders know when to move forward by being visionary and proactive, even in times of difficulty. The marginal leader will sometimes survive in an aura of complacency, but when the storm hits, he or she may well get swept away in the fury of change. An effective leader will always be vigilant to the needs of the institution and rarely lacks the motivation to make tough decisions. Once again, the leader must look at what is in the best interest of the institution, make the decision with a clear conscience, and be prepared for the next decision that inevitably is looming on the horizon.

Summary

A leader's limitations can create problems in decision making, manifested as barriers. Those mentioned are not intended to be all-inclusive, but rather a broadly suggestive list that demonstrates different ways the leader can have his or her decision making clouded by intrinsic and extrinsic forces. A transformational leader realizes that numerous obstacles can cloud positive and fundamental decision making, yet makes decisions based on what is in the best interest of the institution.

Conceptual Framework

Do you see yourself objectively? Do you understand and acknowledge your own limitations? Consider the following questions:

1. Do you lead in immoral, unethical, or illegal ways? To do so erodes trust. Trust is essential to sound decision making. How do you build trust?

2. Do you have addictions that could affect decision making?

3. Do you possess character or personality traits that could potentially limit decision making? This might include lying, cheating, sarcasm, lack of work ethic, arrogance, or fear.

4. Do you lead from a "me first" orientation? Do you regularly consider yourself before the common good when making decisions?

5. Are you easily influenced by "power people"? Can the power of connections, money, property, or knowledge influence decisions for the common good?

6. Do you frequently make decisions from the heart? Are common sense and objective evidence often overlooked when making decisions because you know differently in your heart?

7. Can you explain difficult decisions? The answer is likely "yes" if your decisions are aligned with the vision and mission of the institution and institutional stakeholders were involved in the decisions. Additionally, the vision and mission must be aligned with other interdependent institutions.

8. Do you fear negative stakeholder reactions to difficult decisions? Have you acted improperly, or not at all, in an effort to minimize the impact of a difficult decision? Considering the common good when making difficult decisions minimizes fear.

9. Is your decision making aligned with the institution's vision and mission? Is there stakeholder buy-in for the vision and mission?

10. Do you lack the resolve to make tough decisions?

Reflective Thinking

1. Describe a recent example in which you led from the heart. How did this influence your decision making? How was the heart orientation a strength and a limitation?

2. You have 30 seconds to describe your institution's vision and mission—Go! Can you easily articulate the vision and mission? Can other stakeholders in your institution? What is the role of the vision and mission in your decision making?

3. Describe an example of a "me first" orientation that eroded effective decision making. What was the selfish motive? How did it affect the decision?

4

Overcoming External Barriers to Decision Making

The moment we break faith with one another,
the sea engulfs us and the light goes out.

—James Baldwin

U ndoubtedly, there will be educational scenarios that seemingly confound the theory of transformational decision making. Furthermore, it should be acknowledged that decisions are rarely black and white, clear or opaque, or certain or unsure. Most decisions fall somewhere along a continuum between these extremes. Some instances will require decisions that are somewhat hazy in terms of objectivity, or confoundedly uncertain when diverse perspectives are considered. This is the competing dimension of educational decision making for school leaders. In other words, school leaders often gain ground with one decision, only to lose ground elsewhere as a result of the decision. For example, a school leader who dedicates resources to professional development may have reduced direct instructional teacher-student time as a result of professional development activities and expended revenue toward activities that otherwise might have been used for wages or wage-related benefits. This competing dimension should not imply the decision was wrong; it is simply a decision competing with other demands. These instances will be explored in this chapter to help leaders identify the barriers to clear leadership decision making. However, an enlightened leader who shares the principles of transformational thinking with stakeholders and practices the pedagogy of transformational decision making will experience a transformation of effectiveness that is positive and productive. The contemporary leader will find decision making much easier and clearer for the benefit of all stakeholders, even when barriers manifest themselves as leadership dilemmas.

The following four barriers can place enormous pressures on the decision-making process. Some of these items persist as influences affecting decision making beyond a leader's control. Inherent to the complex system of education are circumstances that place a leader in a compromised position.

1. Prevailing laws and organizational guidelines dictate transformational decision making.

2. Prevailing sociopolitical pressures strongly influence the decision-making process.

3. Media or other communication pressures disrupt sound, transformational decision making.

4. A looming decision may not exhibit any clear-cut path to what is in the best interest of the institution. The decision may be so clouded that a clear transformational decision may be impossible to determine.

Prevailing laws and organizational guidelines dictate transformational decision making. Often, federal, state, or local policy mandates will outweigh building and district initiatives or priorities. This is inherent to the governance structure of public schooling. Laws, codes, policy, and guidelines are often put into place to protect the educational rights of individuals or groups of individuals. In these cases, the institution must comply. State versus local educational control is an excellent example of broader educational mandates overriding local preference. On issues of state control, it is assumed there is a good faith effort to further a free and appropriate constitutional commitment to educating all students. However, this is often at the expense of some local control. Because locale and other demographic characteristics distinguish local communities and their schools, institutions may interpret issues of state and federal control as barriers to sound decision making regarding teaching and learning. The transformational leader simply factors these variables into the decision-making process, and the result will be a decision that reflects these mandates in a productive way.

Prevailing sociopolitical pressures strongly influence the decision-making process. This country, with its unlimited media resources, information technologies, and ever-improving educated populace, creates scenarios that reveal strong societal pressures to act in certain ways or to make certain decisions. Local, state, and federal politics can manifest themselves in similar ways. Enormous pressures are placed on leaders to act in sociopolitically acceptable ways. A leader who completely ignores these pressures is likely to fail, and the institution that he or she leads could also be compromised. Issues that affect people—such as poverty, homelessness, joblessness, injury, or entitlement—can create pressures on leaders to act in ways that demonstrate isolated decision making. To not be responsive to these pressures might appear undemocratic or unethical. Yet making decisions based solely on isolated sociopolitical pressures can be harmful to transformational decision making. If a decision has profound sociopolitical implications, the contemporary leader must consider the fallout. If a decision is required, even with compelling outside pressure to bear, a great leader will gather all pertinent, objective information or evidence and act accordingly. A powerful illustration of this is a district that needs new and improved facilities. Although the institution may have adhered to a strong "form follows function" philosophy, external stakeholders may want taxing impact to be the first and foremost consideration. Strong leaders will consider all perspectives and resist sociopolitical pressures, allowing taxing impact to not suppress objective and compelling educational need.

Media and other communication pressures disrupt sound, transformational decision making. At first, people believed that the media simply reported educational news. In recent years, there is a growing belief that the media and other communication outlets (e.g., the Internet) *create* educational news. News coverage can be wrought with biased opinion, subjective data, anecdotal information, editorialization, and the use of anonymous sources. Media sources have been accused of not just reporting the news, but actually creating and interpreting it for consumers of information. Regardless of one's opinion, the media and other communication brokers are profoundly powerful and cannot be taken lightly. Leaders must never forget the power of the media and other communication sources for their positive and negative contributions. Positive reporting by the media will rarely doom a leader or the institution he or she represents. However, the unpredictable nature of information reporting, which often lacks a viable check system to ensure objectivity, can spell disaster for leaders of scrutinized institutions. The contemporary leader calculates the impact that the media or other communication outlets will have on a particular decision when it is important to do so. The leader must then factor this barrier into decision making and base decisions on what is in the best interest of the institution. The media and other information providers can hinder the positive effects of a transformational decision, even when the decision was made with sound pedagogy and objective information as its basis. Unfortunately, the media and other information outlets have become the single biggest power broker of knowledge and knowledge creation in the world today. Even governmental institutions are rivaled in power by the media. The leader who ignores this fact can hinder the institution he or she serves. The media and other information brokers can serve leaders well, but these same sources can wreak havoc on sound transformational decision making.

A looming decision may not exhibit any clear-cut path to what is in the best interest of the institution. The decision may be so clouded that a clear transformational decision may be impossible to determine. This barrier, although a frequent influence on transformational decision making, is far less threatening than the others. Sometimes, a leader cannot find a clear path to decision making even after gathering data or evidence, gaining diverse perspectives, and remaining objective. These are occasions when the decision seems clouded, with no clearly defined direction. Occasionally, a leader will be faced with a decision that seems equally good or bad, equally clear or opaque, and similarly clear or unclear with competing directions seemingly just as feasible. And sometimes, a leader will see things squarely in the middle regarding which decision to make. If the leader can find no clear, compelling path to decide a certain way, then he or she must look at historical data, use past experience, consider the institutional culture, and employ instinct to act in decisive ways that best serve the common good. Once the decision is made, the contemporary leader monitors closely the decision's impact, keeping in mind that a modification of the decision may be necessary. Usually, a tough decision with no compelling direction to take will most likely work out in positive ways for the institution if implementation of the decision remains a leadership focus. Based on implementation success, the leader may eventually see a clearing of the path for future decision making.

When a decision *must* be made for the good of the institution, regardless of outcome, the leader must act decisively and confidently. Even the appearance of indecisiveness and a lack of confidence can erode decision making with doubt. Transformational leaders must act, accept responsibility, and remain flexible with regard to the original decision as implementation of the decision unfolds.

Consider the example of a high school with an open campus for lunch. To close the campus would certainly improve safety and security for students during the school day. Alternatively, it would hinder businesses that have relied on lunch sales, potentially require capital expenditures to create a cafeteria or commons to handle the increased school lunch business, and challenge a community culture that has afforded its high school students the freedom of an open campus. This culture likely will be resistant to change if an open-campus concept is viewed as a crucial step in post–high school maturation. It becomes even more difficult if the decision is not driven by a significant event (e.g., a student who was injured as a result of driving off campus at lunch or frequent acts of student misconduct throughout the community during lunchtime). The decision may be gray and confounded by diverse perspectives. A proper course is to consider multiple perspectives, collect all objective data or evidence available, take into consideration all confounding barriers, and simply decide in the best interest of the common good.

Summary

A leader must serve the institution objectively, collecting as much evidence as possible from as many sources as possible before making a decision. When barriers confound the process, a prudent leader will simply factor in these obstacles as another consideration in the decision-making process. Having considered all variables, the leader must act in ways that further the institution best. By minimizing the effects of confounding variables, the leader can ensure the best decision and minimize the competing nature of decisions. Hopefully, the barriers will not erode institutional efforts. When the barriers are so persuasive and profoundly influential, good leaders rely on capacities within the institution to minimize impact (e.g., tight value structure and loose culture) rather than mandating short-term solutions inconsistent with the common good and sound decision-making pedagogy.

Conceptual Framework

Leaders must consider the external influences that might leverage their decisions.

1. Do you have internal capacities for change? In other words, can your institution change? If not, how can you build change capacity into the institutional culture?

2. Does your institution have a tight value structure? In other words, can it articulate its educational identity? Tight values can sustain external influences that are not aligned with the institution's vision and mission.

3. Do you and your institutional stakeholders believe that you are all in control of teaching and learning? If not, who is? Institutions must believe they are in control of teaching and learning, even when faced with persistent external pressures. Transformational leaders model this.

4. How do you respond to sociopolitical influences such as poverty, homelessness, high-stakes accountability, and diversity? Are there politically correct responses? Are there undemocratic responses?

5. Are the media your educational community's main source of information for institutional decisions? If so, is this a strength or a limitation? How are decisions communicated? What other means of communication could you pursue?

6. What do you consider when a clear-cut decision cannot be made? Consider multiple perspectives, available evidence, competing influences, and the common good.

Reflective Thinking

1. Identify external influences that place enormous pressures on your decision making.

2. In what ways do the media influence decisions in your institution? How would you define your current media relations?

3. Healthy institutions are often defined as having a tight value structure and loose culture (i.e., can easily adapt and change). What values define your institution? How would you describe your institutional culture?

5

Aligning Decision Making to the Leader's Mission

Nothing will work unless you do.

—Maya Angelou

Effective leaders know that acting in isolation or issuing top-down mandates can be detrimental. Clearly, the effective leader guides the institution toward a collaborative alignment of vision and mission. Beyond the many ways to build consensus and develop strong directional visioning and missioning, transformational leaders ultimately must make decisions once this process has been completed. Effective leaders can answer the following question: "How do I make decisions once the collaborative alignment of vision and mission within the institution has taken place?" The answer to this question has much to do with leadership gifts and talents, key stakeholders, institutional structure, and the valuing of stakeholder importance.

Effective institutional structure dictates that leaders must, among other things, be hard working, visible, articulate, and moral; exhibit great people skills; garner effective management skills; and be visionary. Do leaders exhibiting these lofty leadership traits exist in numbers that allow institutions to have choices in their selection of leaders? The answer is yes, no, and maybe! Thousands of educational leaders have these skills and are serving in positions of leadership at all institutional levels. Without question, not all of these skills are equally necessary to lead every institution that exists. Institutions are as unique as the people who comprise them. Each institution will determine the critical attributes necessary for effective leadership. Each leader possesses a unique set of gifts and talents that encompasses a diverse array of attributes. Simply stated, leaders should serve institutions that have needs that align with their gifts and talents. This should be the primary criterion used in matching institutions with leaders. Regardless of the hiring process used, leader selection must be grounded in the best interests of the institution. Consider nothing else.

Every human has challenges and strengths. It is imperative that leaders understand their own challenges and build capacities in the institution that compensate for this. Great leaders seek out other people who will make the institution shine, not make the leader shine. When a leader decides which person is right for a specific role in the institution, he or she must always view the prospective stakeholder in terms of how this person best suits the institutional role he or she will fill. In other words, how does the person fit in relationship to the institution? Complementing leadership and the common good is best for the institution. Some leaders may select individuals who make them shine, can be controlled, are overly subordinate, are merely likeable, or are relatives or close friends. All of these reasons are flawed and can destroy sound decision making. A transformational leader should select employees by making sure the institution is furthered by the choice. If an employee will work closely with the leader, he or she must complement existing leadership, allow the institution to shine, and ensure the decision-making nucleus remains strong and powerful.

Simply stated, the transformational leader should select people as employees based on how they will help the institution. When a leader selects people in roles that require a close working relationship with the leader, individuals should be selected who make the overall leadership whole. This is good for the institution. Never select members or employees based on making someone look good or feel good, or doing someone a favor. These appointments create a "good ol' boy" culture that can destroy good institutional structure and hinder the efficient running of any institution.

The mission (i.e., the roadmap to achieve the vision) of the leader is to align the institution toward a common vision (i.e., the dream). Once the vision has been adopted, the leader's resolve is to ensure the vision is articulated and carried out to completion, keeping a proactive role of flexibility. In-flight changes in operations may become necessary, but the "umbrella of vision" must be kept intact. Any distraction from the vision must be considered a simple detour on the way to getting back on the mission's main road. Once the vision is embedded in the climate and culture, the largest single institutional challenge is to simply act in transformational ways. Follow this script of successful decision making and the institution will thrive.

Many people confuse hierarchy of structure with hierarchy of importance and input. This can be clarified by stating that hierarchies of structure are inherent in institutions on grounds of efficiency and accountability. Hierarchies of structure in an institution might be thought of in terms of an upside-down wedding cake, in which the smaller layers of cake, or institutions, are accountable to the larger layers of cake, or institutions. The higher the layer, the more the transformational decision making takes priority over lower layers. If everyone in the institution understands pedagogically how decisions are made, then order, rationale, and collective reasoning behind transformational decisions can prevail. Complete agreement will not always follow, but respect for decision making will be garnered in understanding how the decision was made. Leaders do not have to defend hierarchy or layers, as many people would suggest. It is good and necessary to have layered hierarchy in decision making within school institutions. This layering satisfies the social, political, economic, legal, and cultural contexts of public education. When institutions are aligned, hierarchy is a strength rather than a limitation.

The hierarchy of importance is a completely different phenomenon. Everyone in an institution must be valued equally. Transformational leaders must build capacities in which everyone feels valued and equally important. This can be hard when our society attaches status to job titles. Schools, for example, often distinguish their staff as either certified or noncertified. However, noncertified occupations and the people who work in these jobs are just as important as certified jobs in an institution. In order for an institution to work effectively and efficiently, all occupations must be valued and revered. It is highly advisable for transformational leaders to have direct communications with as many people in the institution as can reasonably be accomplished. Peters (1987) suggests that leaders continually walk around, be visible, talk to employees, and have meaningful conversations with everyone in the organization. This not only creates capacities for stakeholders of an institution to feel valued, it gives the leader valuable feedback opportunities needed to run an institution successfully. Transformational leaders insist that institutions value the importance of all employees. Leaders must also employ methodologies and strategies that create venues to listen to not only employees, but also all stakeholders, to help the institution achieve its vision. Stakeholders will have fabulous ideas that need to be heard and acted upon. Mechanisms and procedures must be implemented to ensure that everyone has an institutional voice.

The hierarchy of decision making can create competing outcomes. This can be overcome by building capacities within the institution that encourage input from all levels. This is not to say leaders should have an open door at all times (i.e., being unconditionally available to all stakeholders at all times). Open-door policies can upset the hierarchy of effective leadership by not encouraging decision making at the lowest institutional level. A partial open door works best by encouraging input at the most appropriate level while remaining accessible. For example, a district leader may want to set aside one day a month to engage in discussion and dialogue with individual school stakeholders. When necessary, the district leader should encourage stakeholders to share input with the most appropriate person, if it has not been previously done.

Summary

Effective leaders must be able to answer the following question: "How do I make decisions once the collaborative alignment of vision and mission within the institution has taken place?" The answer to this question will be as unique as the stakeholders comprising the institution, but must be grounded in the gifts and talents of institutional stakeholders and reflective of the institutional structure. Decision making also requires that hierarchy of structure not be confused with hierarchy of importance and input. Hierarchies of structure are inherent in institutions on grounds of efficiency and accountability, but the hierarchy of importance or input is a completely different phenomenon in which everyone in an institution must be valued equally.

Conceptual Framework

Earlier, you were challenged to ensure that your institution had a meaningful vision and mission that was aligned with interdependent institutions. However, as you work on this decision-making imperative, you must also build capacities for the following considerations:

1. When hiring or adding to the institutional membership, would you consider someone who complements you, or complements the institution? New hires must have an institutional fit, not an existing leadership void fit. Otherwise, the common good is marginalized.

2. Considering institutions through the metaphor of an upside-down wedding cake implies that larger institutional decisions may have priority over smaller institutions. Can you lead in this context? Alignment with other interdependent institutions minimizes issues of precedence.

3. Do you value equally the contributions of all institutional stakeholders? Everyone must feel equally valued and important. In doing so, meaningful input may be solicited from all, ensuring informed decision making.

Reflective Thinking

1. Do you have an open-door or partial open-door communication policy? What other means do you use to encourage and gather stakeholder input?

2. Are faculty (e.g., teachers) more important than staff (e.g., custodians)? Are faculty valued more than staff by school-community stakeholders?

3. Can you think of an example in which a leader's gifts and talents did not align with the needs of the institution? What was the outcome? What implications does this have for you or stakeholders in your institution? What are the recruitment and retention implications?

6

Understanding How Human Nature Affects Decision Making

*A good head and a good heart
are always a formidable combination.*

—Nelson Mandela

In order for leaders to make effective decisions, they must understand what we believe to be 11 general propositions about the nature of human beings (Brower & Balch, 2004). People can place enormous pressures or even subtle and persistent pressures on leaders regarding decision making. A transformational leader must understand the human behaviors behind these pressures and be ever cognizant of the impact these "laws" can have on his or her decision making. Understanding these fundamental laws will help contemporary leaders in their quest to make outstanding decisions for their respective institutions. The following is a list of 11 human nature traits, not intended to be mutually exclusive or all-inclusive. These traits are encountered by school leaders and exhibited consistently by stakeholders of educational institutions.

1. It is always about me.

2. People believe they are doing the right thing and doing a good job.

3. Defining moments clarify and reveal relationships.

4. People desire to leave a lasting legacy.

5. It takes a significant event to change fundamental values and beliefs.

6. People are fundamentally good.

7. The soul does not age.

8. People want to be liked and accepted.

9. People have similar basic needs.

10. People make mistakes.

11. People are influenced by the "law of firsts."

It is always about me. Mr. Landon Scott, a middle school teacher, also served as a middle school team leader. Mr. Scott, on behalf of the team, regularly complained overtly that the school's discipline was "out of control" and worse than at any other time in his teaching career. The principal, Dr. Kim Burdett, responded to the concern by convening a committee whose charge was to develop a systemic discipline plan. Dr. Burdett shared the decisions of the committee with school stakeholders and found some resistance to the plan. Soon after, a group of teachers met with the principal to share its concerns. The points of contention involved those aspects that changed expectations at the classroom and team levels. For example, teachers were expected to call a student's parent or guardian prior to an office referral. Additionally, the team was to conduct a student-parent meeting prior to an office visit. As discussion with the group of teachers ensued, it was clear that the teachers wanted Dr. Burdett and her assistant principal to make parent calls and conduct student-parent meetings. Mr. Scott, a member of the concerned group, noted that teachers were hired to teach and administrators were hired to discipline. Dr. Burdett responded by stating that out-of-control discipline was merely a symptom of a larger root cause. She also reminded the teachers that adding additional steps to office referrals merely moved more control for discipline from the classroom or team to the office, minimizing the control inherent to teachers for discipline issues. Finally, she reaffirmed that the discipline committee had been entrusted to make decisions regarding a difficult issue, and its decisions supported the common good and were aligned with the school's vision and mission. As such, the committee's decisions would stand, with ongoing evaluation during implementation of the discipline plan.

Resistance to change is often immersed in a "me first" orientation. This destructive trait can thwart decisions based on the common good and maintain a focus on symptomatic issues rather than root causes.

This may well be the most important law of human nature that leaders must recognize and understand in order to be an effective leader with transformational decision-making abilities. Abundant evidence exists that this nation has developed into, and continues to be, a "me first" society (Beck, 1998; Dore, 1995; Miel, 1996). Stakeholders of education often determine their acceptance of, rejection of, agreement with, or disagreement with decisions based on how that decision will affect them. If a leader is not aware of this fundamental law of human nature, decision making will be based on what is best for individuals and not what is best for the institution. Ultimately, decisions that are in the best interest of the institution will be in the best interest of institutional stakeholders. However, some stakeholders may be uncomfortable with or experience anxiety over decisions with which they do not agree. This is a predictable outcome and not something that should adversely influence a leader's decision making. Stakeholders can place enormous pressures on leaders to avoid the negative personal impact of a decision. Not only can these pressures be external to the institution (e.g., a local patron), but they can also come from within.

Sometimes, this human nature law can be self-imposed by the leader, who makes a decision based on self-interest. Decisions of self-interest could include job security, increased salary, less work, better benefits, less travel, less stress, or less anxiety. Great leaders recognize this tendency of human nature in others and themselves. Leaders need to be aware of this fundamental law of human nature in order to maintain the integrity of proper decision making and ensure an institutional focus.

People believe they are doing the right thing and doing a good job. Understanding this fundamental law of human nature will help the contemporary leader comprehend and adequately assess why others disagree with the leader's position even when the leader's position seems appropriate and forthright. Consider a teachers' union that believes a 5% pay raise is justified in a contract dispute when the administration's position is to not offer a raise. Both groups have the same information, yet are steadfast in their positions, each offering evidence-based justifications with great confidence. The union representatives might believe the information supports a raise for their membership, and management representatives might believe the same information dictates that any raise would be fiscally irresponsible. Another good example of this fundamental law of human thinking at work was the decision to build the Eiffel Tower in Paris, France. The decision to build this monstrous iron structure was met with strong resistance. The nearly 1,000-foot iron structure, designed by architect Alexander Eiffel, eventually was built solely for the World's Fair Exhibition of 1896. After the fair, many Parisians wanted the structure torn down because they felt it was not an appropriate structure that was in keeping with the history and traditions of Parisian architecture. Ultimately, the Eiffel Tower remained and has helped Paris and France become a major tourist attraction, thus benefiting the many institutions both represent. All stakeholders of the tower, whether for or against its existence, believed they were acting on good faith and for the common good.

Great leaders understand that people often approach decision making and position statements from a framework that they are doing the right thing, for the right reasons, and for the right people. This can be confounding to the decision-making process by leaders of institutions. So, what is a leader to do to protect the decision-making process from this fundamental law of human nature? First, the leader must be cognizant of this potential barrier and the attendant pressures it can exert on decision making. Second, the leader must encourage meaningful input as part of information gathering. This might include sound, objective data and evidence. This can also include qualitative/quantitative research, empirical data and other forms of valid evidence, action research or original research, the wisdom of others, input from diverse institutional stakeholders, and a clear and compelling answer to the question "What is in the best interest of the institution?" A leader must minimize subjectivity in his or her thinking to ensure quality decision making and minimize the "right thing" orientation. Focusing on objectivity in decision making ensures transformational thinking; relying on subjectivity in decision making corrupts this pedagogical thinking and encourages a "right thing" orientation.

Defining moments clarify and reveal relationships. Mr. Steve Barkley was a 26-year veteran social studies teacher who routinely embarrassed his principal in front of other teachers in faculty meetings. Steve's previous principal allowed these embarrassing questions and comments to pass with a shrug or by ignoring the questions and comments. When Mr. Bob Sanchez took over as principal, he had been warned by the assistant principal to be ready for another one of Steve's ill-placed questions or comments.

At the first faculty meeting, Bob was going over the restroom supervision assignments when Steve blurted out that "unlike administrators, I didn't go to college to watch kids going to the bathroom." The faculty sat in stunned silence, waiting to see how the new principal would handle this situation. Bob simply said, "Steve, that question will be answered in my office at the conclusion of this meeting." Bob went on with the meeting and was not interrupted by Steve again. When Steve entered his office, Bob asked him to have a seat. Here is exactly what Bob said. "Steve, let me make one thing perfectly clear to you. I will never embarrass you in front of students, faculty members, or in front of parents. In fact, I will never conscientiously [*sic*] embarrass you. You have a reputation for this behavior, and I was warned that you might do this during my tenure as principal. Now that I have given you my promise, here is what I expect from you. You will not ask a question of me in an attempt to embarrass me. I want to make this very clear to you. I will not tolerate this behavior, nor will I condone it. If you have a legitimate concern at future faculty meetings, you may raise it in a civil manner. Should this happen again, I will consider it grounds for insubordination." Bob went on to say that he hoped they could work together and encouraged Steve to meet with him at any time to share concerns.

This was Bob's defining moment with Steve. Leaders hope they never have to have defining moments, but when it is deemed necessary, effective leaders seize these defining moments.

Not all relationships must have defining moments, but many relationships are framed by particular situations that clarify and reveal parameters later used as a venue to push, pull, stay the course, retreat, launch an offensive, or allow others to move in and make the decision for the leader. A teacher who willfully disregards the decision of a principal is a prime example of a teacher-administrator defining moment. The teacher will likely understand the consequences of this decision, but if the administrator capitulates and allows the teacher to disregard an educational directive, the teacher could likely continue to push the limits of compliance until a future defining moment determines the boundaries. This can gravely influence decision making. When a defining moment never materializes as in the preceding example, the institution suffers. Stakeholders think twice before disregarding a transformational leader or negatively influencing decision making if the leader has had a significant, defining, and clarifying moment with the person in an earlier encounter. Defining moments were not intended to encourage ill feelings or consequences; rather, they are a "draw a line in the sand" approach to what will and will not be accepted or tolerated in a professional relationship when the need arises.

Great leaders understand the need to act decisively to determine appropriate boundaries for future decision making. Many times, a difficult decision that creates a defining moment will make future decisions not only easier, but more clarifying to those whom the decision affects. Establishing these professional parameters soundly defines institutional relationships.

People desire to leave a lasting legacy. Leaders and many institutional stakeholders are driven to leave a lasting legacy for the generations that follow them. As leaders professionally mature, they begin to garner an identity. This identity is generally representative of the gifts and talents a leader is contributing to education. However, as the identity grows and becomes a source of pride, it can influence a leader's decision making and thinking. Some leaders are so driven to leave a legacy that it can negatively affect sound decision making.

Superintendent Beau Michaels, for example, takes great pride in helping communities build schools and other educational facilities. Beau believes his professional identity is that of a "building-builder," and he is convinced that sound teaching and learning can occur only in state-of-the art contemporary facilities. Beau is willing to further his legacy of "form follows function" at the expense of other priorities. Beau's leadership frequently divides communities, and his professional identity is often tied directly to construction and renovation projects. He responds by stating that "needs are many and competing; however, other issues cannot be sufficiently addressed until the educational facilities are improved." Beau finds himself changing jobs rather frequently, seeking other districts in need of new facilities. He is willing to accept this as his plight, given his "true" gifts and talents.

Great leaders must resist the urge to leave a legacy that clouds sound decision making. Leaders must always make decisions by asking, "What is in the best interest of the institution?" Keeping this question in mind as a framework for decision making will maximize clarity in decision making. Wanting to leave a legacy not only creates problems in decision making, but also creates a torrent of destruction. Another example might be a corporation that decides to purchase energy management services under the guise of improving efficiency. The leader of the corporation may provide a persuasive argument for school board members, but the underlying motive might be to retire from the corporation with this feather in his or her cap and an energy management consulting job. The result might end up a capital expenditure waste for personal gain. If the decisions were made entirely in the best interest of the institution and not for the leader's legacy, then the decision was the appropriate one. The reasons are critical to determine if the decision is proper. Leaders must be aware of this trap of human behavior to adequately assess what is right for the institution and not what is right for the leader's legacy.

It takes a significant event to change fundamental values and beliefs. Tonya Miracle, Director of Guidance at a suburban high school, was asked to provide recommendations to the School Improvement Committee regarding the role of parents in the overall school improvement process. Tonya's expertise had been sought because her small group and individual counseling was excellent. Furthermore, her career and postgraduation guidance was exemplary. As a part of her guidance and counseling duties, Tonya had dealt with parents for many years. For Tonya, parents had been a source of frustration. In fact, she had often commented to the other counselors that dealing with parents "wasn't her thing." She often lamented, "Schools only have these kids a few hours each day—what can we do? Parents have the greatest influence."

When Tonya made a presentation to the School Improvement Committee, the message was clear: Schools aren't the problem, parents are. Furthermore, Tonya reported that schools have little influence over parents, so the best we can do is figure out how to make a difference in the short time we have the students at school. Tonya abruptly ended the presentation by throwing her arms in the air, exclaiming, "I'm sorry there aren't better solutions, but this is our reality."

The committee was shocked and dismayed. This led to a broader discussion and the appointment of a parent advisory committee whose charge was to provide home-school recommendations. Eventually, several ideas were shared with the School Improvement Committee. These included, in part, school-based mental health services for families, a useful and up-to-date Web site, student-led parent-teacher conferences, and more frequent assessment feedback from teachers to parents.

As school accountability expectations heightened, so did the teaching and learning role for Tonya and her department. Tonya, however, continued to believe educators had little control over teaching and learning as it related to parents. Soon, other school stakeholders were celebrating strengthened parent-school relationships, and overall assessment scores were improving as a result of these efforts. Yet Tonya continued to dismiss it as a fluke and something that would never be sustained over time. Eventually, Tonya was replaced with a guidance counselor having a long history of family advocacy and a fundamental belief in systemic parent involvement. It was only after Tonya was reassigned and considering her professional future that she began to reflect on her role in a parent-school plan. She now longed to reevaluate her position on home-school connections and the role they play in school improvement.

Fundamental values and beliefs that leaders develop over time are instrumental in decision making. Many times, these values and beliefs help the leader make good, sound decisions, but sometimes, these values and beliefs can negatively affect a leader's vision for sound decision making. Leaders must discipline themselves to look beyond their own personal values and beliefs and view the landscape of the institution from a more unbiased and objective viewpoint. As difficult as it may seem at times for the leader to shift values and beliefs, a great leader understands this fundamental law of human nature and is compelled to remain flexible, challenging his or her own beliefs and values absent a significant event.

Changing these values and beliefs can be nearly impossible without the leader developing a disciplined, open mind. Evidence would suggest that fundamental changes in people's value and belief systems require profound, life-changing events—being fired, demoted, or promoted in a career; getting a divorce; having children; losing a loved one; having an accident; and radically altering or changing one's lifestyle through moving, changing careers, and/or children moving away. All of these profound changes can have impacts on decision making; not all are negative, and some can even be positive. Nevertheless, inflexible values and beliefs can negatively affect good, sound decision making. The transformational leader is cognizant of the potential impact of this type of influence on transformational decision making. Great leaders do not wait for profound, life-changing events to influence values and beliefs; they focus on the common good to shape core values and beliefs.

For example, a teacher who has taught only in a rural setting and is suddenly immersed in an urban setting may find his or her values and beliefs inconsistent with the new institution's core values and beliefs. This teacher may need to embrace a value and belief system that is completely foreign in order to enjoy success in this new setting. The informed leader will see these situations for what they are: conflicting values and beliefs. A transformational leader of any institution is aware of this potentially fatal barrier and adjusts to situations in flexible, open-minded ways. Transformational leaders do not let personal values and beliefs destroy what is in the best interest of the institution.

People are fundamentally good. Anna Gonzalez was a long-time middle school math teacher in a suburban school district. She had recently finished her administrative degree through the district's groom-your-own program. Soon after program completion, the human resources director contacted Anna about an administrative opening in a middle school elsewhere in the district. She eagerly pursued the opportunity and was offered the position of assistant principal. Part of her new duties included the supervision of teachers with greater than 5 years of experience. Anna, as a long-time faculty member in the district, had heard stories of the teachers she would soon evaluate. Some of the "old guard," she had heard, were selfish, burned out, or simply incompetent. Armed with current evaluation knowledge and skills from her administrative program, she prepared to tackle the evaluation list. The bargained agreement limited her evaluation options, but it did afford her multiple classroom visits. While conducting visitations, she soon found the "old guard" teachers had many gifts and talents to share; the teaching and learning she had observed needed to be acknowledged and celebrated, not marginalized by demeaning labels. In fact, her instructional leadership had improved as a result of her visitations and subsequent teacher conferences. As Anna's leadership identity began to emerge, she found herself advocating for the gifts and talents of all teachers, using evaluation as a means of assisting all faculty in achieving their potential. When disparaging remarks were made about "old guard" teachers, or any other inappropriate label to characterize the professionals in her school, she was quick to challenge the label and champion the meaningful contributions made by all of her faculty.

All people are basically good . . . it is a fundamental law of human nature. As such, all leaders are basically good, too. Descriptors such as *good* are often used to generally describe an individual, but labeling people with general descriptors can impose limitations by describing complex individuals narrowly and leaving interpretation of the label to bias. However, it is a reality of human nature to label people. As unproductive as the practice of labeling can be, it nevertheless happens daily in our lives. Furthermore, when looking at institutions, general descriptive labels are equally inappropriate. Institutions should not be labeled with general descriptors. Labels like *good, bad, biased, inviting, uncaring, wise, efficient, moral,* or other similar descriptions cannot define an institution. Labels are more descriptive and accurate when describing particular events or the actions of individuals. Furthermore, actions and events are likely the result of decision making. For example, a label can identify the actions of an individual making a poor choice, a bad decision, a wise move, or an ethical alternative. These same labels should not be used to describe a complete individual unless they can be articulated through a composite of actions or decision outcomes. A composite of great decisions might warrant describing someone as an outstanding leader. Others might describe these same decisions as selfish, indecisive, and unwarranted. General descriptors are largely subjective and left to individual interpretation. So, what tips the balance between descriptors such as *good* and *evil, bias* and *acceptance, love* and *hate, caring* and *not caring*? There is no tipping of the balance to describe people or leaders in general terms except for individual interpretation; however, labels focused on specific actions or events, or composites of actions and events, are more meaningful, more representative, and less vulnerable to a host of biased interpretations. For example, a district leader might make a series of decisions that empowers teachers and students toward improved learning, but requires an increase in local taxes. Some might describe the leader as an outstanding instructional leader, whereas others could describe the same leader as exorbitant and wasteful. So, what is the answer? Avoid general labeling of people or institutions. When one uses transformational thinking, the only criterion used to evaluate the leader and other institutional stakeholders will be the answer to the question, "Has the individual's action resulted in what is best for the institution he or she serves?"

To further clarify and describe this concept, one need only observe an expulsion hearing. The observer might witness a student being removed from school for a lengthy term because of a shocking act, only to have family members and other witnesses expound on all the good qualities this student possesses. Family or friends of the student might note this one shocking incident as a temporary error in judgment that should be forgiven, regardless of the legal context, because of the many good things this same student has done for others at some point in time. Why is this? How can a person be good and bad at the same time, depending on a person's viewpoint? The answer lies in labeling. Labels are highly personal and represent only one person's subjective viewpoint. It is best to refrain from using labels to generally describe any person. What is good to one person may be bad to another . . . it is always personal and subjective. So, leaders must minimize the use of labels at all times.

Institutions should not be described with labels because they exist only in artificial terms. Actions and events can have these labels, but even they remain open to subjectivity. This is a significant paradigm shift in thinking for the decision-making leader. Most leaders are familiar with descriptive labels such as *good* and *bad* and how they are used to describe institutions, but these labels are simply misplaced. Labels have been used to describe nearly all institutions at some time or another. These generalized descriptive labels are unproductive and inappropriate because institutions are incapable of feeling or thinking. Institutions exist only in artificial terms. Remember, labeling describes actions and events. Schools are not good or bad—only the actions or events related to school stakeholders in the school can be described as good or bad.

General labeling of individuals and institutions serves no good purpose! The end result of this common labeling practice ultimately will be counterproductive to an institution. This misguided practice often leads to anxiety that may force unwarranted actions or consequences, destroying the climate and culture of an institution. The transformational leader understands that labels are nearly always destructive when used in general terms. However, the transformational leader continually seeks out the composite of actions and events that support the belief that people are basically good. All humans will make mistakes at some time in their lives. This does not mean these humans are bad, only that they have made a bad choice. Transformational leaders clearly communicate the hazards of labeling and accept that good people will make mistakes. By understanding this fundamental law of human nature, a great leader will make sound decisions based on acts, events, and other sources of evidence, rather than generalized and misguided labels. By looking at facts, staying objective, and not generally labeling individuals, leaders can make clear decisions in the best interest of the institutions they lead.

The soul does not age. Mrs. Kathryn-Elizabeth Barnett, a long-time teacher in a small rural district, was nearing retirement. The new administrator, Mr. Gregory Alan, looked forward to her retirement, yearning to surround himself with teachers who were trained in a standards-based environment. "The problem is," Greg lamented, "Kathryn-Elizabeth teaches with her heart, and that is not what the state is rewarding. I need teachers focused on knowledge and skills." As the academic year gained momentum, Greg led and modeled from an output-based orientation. Evidence was the only consideration for decision making. When the fall semester came to a close, a final faculty meeting remained prior to the seasonal break. The new administrator announced that milk breaks and morning recess would be cancelled, beginning in the spring semester. "More minutes are needed," he rationalized, "for instruction to raise state assessment scores." During the meeting, teachers were asked to provide evidence that increasing instructional minutes was wrong. They were also asked if there was any evidence to consider retaining milk breaks and recess. The room was silent. Finally, in a gentle tone, Kathryn-Elizabeth spoke. "For the many years that I served on this faculty, we've not only been concerned about the knowledge and skills of students, but what they value, believe, and dream about, too. Teachers, too, for that matter, have been able to express what they value, believe, and dream about. Sometimes, a break or recess is necessary simply because it is the right thing to do; something I know in my heart. We're forgetting the heart of education. In doing so, I'm concerned students and faculty alike will lose their enthusiasm for teaching and learning. Knowledge and skills are important, but the heart is, too." As Greg and the faculty listened intently, it was clear the wisdom of the master teacher had provided a critical piece of insight that had been lacking during the fall semester. Consensus quickly formed that additional instructional minutes were necessary, but breaks and recess might be necessary as well. An advisory group was formed to consider multiple options. Greg gained a new respect for Kathryn-Elizabeth and frequently sought her perspective until her retirement.

A leader realizes that time passes insidiously forward. Good leaders understand mortality. Even nonliving things experience a similar phenomenon through some form of change. No matter how good things are or how smoothly things are working, eventually, entities will change despite forces operating to prevent change. Efforts to thwart change, including mortality, have proven unsuccessful.

People change, too. Beyond individual beliefs, one thing is clear about human nature: We do not age on the inside, where our souls reside. Transformational leaders recognize that age does not change the soul of a person. The soul is a place where our values, beliefs, and faiths reside. The soul provides the values-laden portion of teaching, learning, and leading; from the soul emanates the heart of education. Just because someone is aging chronologically does not mean that he or she is unproductive, nor does it assume that he or she cannot make significant contributions to the institution. Transformational leaders know the value of wisdom and experience, and they realize that the soul does not age. Numerous examples exist among school stake-holders who are chronologically older, but young in terms of professional contributions, productivity, and commitment. The soul does not age, and great leaders understand the soul and its perfection. Transformational leaders build on this phenomenon to make great decisions that benefit the institution and, ultimately, the people in the institution; decisions that tap the soul's potential.

People want to be liked and accepted. Dr. Joyce Hart was a district super-intendent who was known as a people pleaser. Joyce took great pride in saying "yes" to nearly all requests. "Why say no if we can say yes?" was her motto. Joyce was so enamored with pleasing people that she forgot to lead with her district's best interests in mind. Her leadership identity lacked focus, and she had become all things to all people. Eventually, she discovered that what was good for one person might not be good for another. This competed with her desire to be liked by all. By trying to please some people, she found she alienated others.

Over time, the common good of the district was compromised, and an individual, selfish focus emerged. No one could articulate the vision and mission of the district because decisions were not aligned with these once-powerful statements. Whoever got to Joyce first usually got what he or she wanted. Because she continually led this way, the district's morale plunged and her leadership was no longer valued. Within 2 years, Joyce used her financial strengths to secure a position as a chief financial officer at a local bank where the motto "the customer is always right" suited her well. Joyce, when reflecting on her superintendency, came to the conclusion that effective leadership is not about fulfilling the desire to be liked or accepted.

Understanding the powerful influences of this law can steer a leader in the right direction when it comes to transformational decision making. If a leader is concerned with being liked by stake-holders of the institution, that can negatively influence good, sound, decision making. Likewise, transformational leaders understand that people within their institutions want to be liked and accepted just as much as the leader has this fundamental need. Leaders must develop the resolve to make the right decision at the expense of being liked. Transformational leaders must make decisions based on what is in the best interest of the institution and not out of concern that someone may not like them or their decisions. Leaders must understand that this fundamental law of human nature can easily sway them to make decisions that are not transformationally sound. Ultimately, if the institution is healthy, the individuals who define the institution will be professionally healthy. Transformational leaders do not let individuals dictate transformational decision making at the expense of the common good. These same leaders also do not let their own desire for acceptance interfere with decisions. If leaders make decisions predicated on what is good for themselves or other individuals in the short run, they risk damaging or destroying the institution they lead. Great transformational leaders understand the long-term benefits of sound decisions versus the short-term trap of being liked and accepted. If leaders are not cognizant of the illusive pressures to please individuals in return for being accepted and liked, they run the risk of hurting far more people within the institution. A great transformational leader does not allow other people's feelings about him or her to personally affect his or her clear-minded decision-making abilities. When leaders act for the good of the institution, they understand that people often base their individual opinions and feelings on highly subjective viewpoints. The subjective viewpoints of some individuals, either internal or external to the institution, may develop into ill feelings toward a leader when not validated through the decision-making process. The transformational leader understands and accepts this phenomenon of human nature. Everyone benefits when a transformational leader's desire to be liked does not permeate thinking and decision making.

People have similar basic needs. Robert Pence had recently accepted district-level duties as a director at a moderately sized school district. Robert was previously an elementary principal who had a history of ineffectiveness with his staff. As a result of his marginal building leadership, Robert was transferred to a new position at the district level.

Robert had a significant limitation in his leadership: He was a "control freak." Robert was a micromanager and constantly meddled in the minutiae of other employees' work. He rarely delegated or empowered others.

Three weeks into his district-level job, the superintendent was fielding complaints from various employees. The superintendent immediately planned a face-to-face meeting with Robert. Robert was asked to explain his behaviors and his leadership style that had alienated so many under his supervision. Robert simply scoffed at the complaints as mere ripples in trying to straighten up a department that was badly in need of "old school" values. It was obvious that Robert felt he was not the source of turmoil in the department. At the conclusion of the meeting, the superintendent had made his expectations clear and believed that the meeting had been productive. Robert left the meeting assuring the superintendent that he would address the concerns immediately. The superintendent was encouraged by Robert's attitude.

Two days later, the assistant director under Robert's supervision notified the superintendent of her immediate resignation. The superintendent was shocked and asked the assistant to sit down and explain her reasoning. The superintendent listened intently to the assistant's unwillingness to be disloyal to her supervisor, but it was obvious that a major dispute between the two had surfaced. The assistant refused to divulge the details of the conflict, but simply said that her resignation would be the first of many if a change in leadership were not forthcoming. A sense of impending doom swept over the superintendent as he began to grasp the severity of his mistake in appointing Robert to this position. Searching for a greater explanation, the superintendent asked if things had improved over the previous two days. The assistant stated, "Oh, we heard about your meeting with Robert . . . things have been terribly difficult around the office since he returned from the meeting with you." The superintendent felt betrayed and bewildered at the same time.

At the superintendent's request, the assistant agreed to rescind the resignation for one week until some resolution to the problem could be made. That afternoon, two more resignations were delivered to the superintendent's office. The superintendent knew that he now would be forced to act on his mistake of appointing Robert to a district-level position. Robert was summoned to the superintendent's office and immediately placed on administrative leave. Robert was given an opportunity to explain his behavior once the evidence had been leveled against him, but he stammered, mumbled, and gave little credible evidence in his own defense. Robert appeared stunned by the allegations against him. Subsequently, he was relieved of all duties. The district later moved to not renew his administrative contract.

Robert had furthered his own needs, manifested as a micromanager, while not considering the needs of his employees. By not considering the needs of others, Robert's leadership was ineffective, and an unhealthy climate quickly ensued. School stakeholders at any level must have a degree of control over their professional practice. Micromanaging strips this control. Stakeholders must also be valued and trusted. Micromanaging sends a devaluing message of distrust. Robert had failed to recognize these fundamental needs.

A need might be considered the lack of something desirable, or to be in want. A large body of scholarship exists on needs and motives (i.e., the actions to obtain a need). For example, Glasser (1986), a renowned medical doctor and educator, describes five fundamental needs that guide human behavior: survival, love, freedom, fun, and control. Glasser claims that thriving organizations are composed of individuals who have these needs fulfilled. Because these needs are basic and universal, it stands to reason that these needs should also be considered rules for understanding basic human behavior. These same human needs help reveal what motivates humans to act in certain ways. Understanding these motivators as they relate to behavior is essential to implementing transformational decision making. Decisions that advance the common good and fulfill needs will be embraced widely, whereas those decisions profiting the common good but not satisfying basic needs may be more challenging and less likely to gain acceptance.

Although Glasser's needs are not mutually exclusive, they provide an example of the insight that exists regarding what motivates people to act and feel a certain way. The five human needs will usually manifest themselves in situations involving people. A leader with this framework of understanding can objectively peel away the layers of individual need, forming a clear vision of what is best for the institution.

In addition to understanding these needs and motivational factors in others, leaders must also acknowledge and understand how these same needs affect their own behavior. A transformational leader can understand and acknowledge his or her needs to accurately assess their impact on decision making. Transformational leaders know themselves to ensure effective decision making. A great leader fully understands that the needs of people can adversely affect sound decision making. Leaders must see objectively, clearly assessing individual needs to make great decisions. They study and understand human needs, including their own, in order to accurately assess decision making. Armed with this objectivity and an understanding of basic needs, leaders are free to make great decisions.

People make mistakes. Tony Peyton was the superintendent of a school corporation with a $22,000,000 annual budget. During his budget-building process for the fiscal year, Tony made a $537,000 revenue error in calculating the general fund debt. At every checkpoint in the budget, the error went unnoticed with devastating results in the generated revenue from the state. The error was discovered a few months into the new budget year when Tony studied percentages of appropriations exceeding similar historical comparisons from previous years. Tony called a special board meeting to inform the board of what he had found. The board expressed concern about the district's impending shortfall and questioned Tony's ability to provide continued fiscal leadership. Soon after the initial meeting, Tony believed his future with the corporation was uncertain. This quickly translated to a state of worry. As Tony reflected on the error and how to move forward, he knew there was only one solution: Tell the truth, fully disclose the error in transparent ways, and accept full responsibility.

Resolutions were sought and solutions were found. During the problem-solving process, board members and other school-community stakeholders observed his forthright handling of the problem and overall professional maturity. Soon after solutions were implemented, the board met privately to discuss Tony's future. The board members felt that Tony's leadership history was solid, and this human error was a mistake that must be forgiven. Tony had built a $2 million cash surplus in the budget since his arrival 3 years earlier, largely due to his expertise in school finance. As a result, the district was in sound financial shape.

During the board president's comment regarding the revenue shortfall at the next regularly scheduled board meeting, she fully explained the fiscal error that had been made, what actions were being undertaken to resolve the shortfall, and that the superintendent accepted full responsibility. Given Tony's professional maturity and truthful disclosure, the school-community accepted the mistake without further consequences. The board moved beyond the error, but challenged Tony to review the budget-building process and ensure that a check-and-balance system existed so the mistake could not be repeated.

One thing is certain in life . . . humans will make mistakes and do wrong things. It is important for leaders to understand this important phenomenon in order to allow others to make mistakes and, likewise, to move forward when the leader makes a mistake. Acknowledging responsibility for a mistake and learning from it is also important and should be encouraged among all institutional stakeholders. If the leader understands this fundamental law of human nature, he or she can make tough decisions confidently absent the nagging anxiety to appear flawless that often accompanies decisions. Armed with this knowledge, a leader can model for others that when a mistake is made, accept responsibility for the mistake, learn from it, and move forward.

This powerful form of modeling combined with transformational thinking will benefit the common good by encouraging individual responsibility and risk taking.

People are influenced by the "law of firsts." Onalee Hite was in her first year as one of several assistant principals for a large urban high school. When Onalee had been on the job only a few days, a foreign language teacher had referred a student to her office for cheating in Spanish class. The teacher produced a rumpled crib sheet as evidence—necessary evidence because the student would not confess to his teacher. Eventually, the guilty student confessed to Onalee, and a 3-day suspension from class ensued. Onalee supported the suspension from class not only because of the cheating infraction, but also because of the student's reaction to the teacher upon being confronted with the accusation.

Although the student initially lied to the teacher about his culpability in the situation, Onalee was able to engender trust in the student and build a relationship that encouraged a confession. Because the issue wasn't resolved until the end of the day and did not include out-of-school exclusion, Onalee did not call the student's parents, believing the young man would explain what happened to his mother. Onalee planned to mail the discipline notice to the parents the following day. Instead, the student discussed a version of the incident with his mother and father, manipulating the story to his benefit. The young man told his parents that he was coerced into confessing to something he had not done. The parents were convinced that the boy was telling the truth.

The next day, both student and parents appeared at school demanding to see the assistant principal. Onalee was shocked by the parents' irate demeanor. Inviting the family into her office, Onalee attempted to calm the parents and looked at Jeremy incredulously. "What did you tell your parents?" was Onalee's first question to the student. The boy expressed to Onalee that he had not cheated on the test and that he wanted to withdraw his confession. Afterwards, the student could not maintain eye contact with Onalee and looked down at the carpet beside the chair. Onalee asked the student to leave her office and to sit in the lobby until she could make sense of what was happening. Onalee then sent for the Spanish teacher and told her the student's parents were in her office.

The parents sat quietly as the teacher explained the course of events from the previous day. At first, the parents found fault with the teacher's version until the actual crib sheet was presented. The parents immediately recognized their son's handwriting and when the tear from the boy's notebook paper matched perfectly with the crib sheet, the parents sat back in their chairs in silence. The parents explored other possible explanations that would exonerate their son, but eventually came to the conclusion that their son had duped them. Finally, they offered an apology and encouraged Onalee to do whatever was necessary in the situation. Onalee excused the teacher from the meeting and tried to comfort the parents. She apologized for not calling the night before. As the parents left and the student returned to the assistant principal's office, Onalee knew she had erred by not calling the parents soon after the discipline had been issued. Fully disclosing the incident, evidence, and outcome first would have been better than trying to do so after the parents had already heard a different version from their child.

Onalee was so intrigued by what had happened that she visited with the principal to share what had transpired. The principal shared several similar stories to illustrate how communicating first is usually a best-practice policy. It was decided to explore ways to improve direct and immediate communication with parents concerning discipline issues.

Leaders want to make decisions with an open mind, but often are influenced by whoever gets to them first. Leaders can be influenced to form opinions quickly, align themselves emotionally, and display a natural tendency to support those who first provide them with compelling evidence.

Transformational leadership requires an awareness of this fundamental law of human nature to ensure that the leader acts rather than reacts. Transformational leadership ignores the temptations inherent in this reactionary behavior. Leaders must always base their decisions on what is in the best interest of the institution and not simply on who gets to them first. The first voice will not be the only voice. Transformational decision making requires that the leader remain objective until information from multiple sources is gathered. Only then can a leader ensure that he or she is acting with transformational thinking as a framework for effective decision making.

Similarly, it should be noted that a great leader must be proactive whenever possible to use the "law of firsts" to favor the institution's common good by being first with information regarding decision making. An enlightened leader can use the "law of firsts" to present information and decisions to stakeholders. Being first will reduce the impact that others can have when they present similar information from a differing viewpoint. If a leader follows this pedagogy of leadership, satisfaction and acceptance of most decisions by those in the institution will ultimately follow.

Summary

The fundamental laws of human nature serve as a driving force for everyone, including leaders. The list of 11 fundamental laws is competing and not mutually exclusive. Great leaders must understand that they are influenced by the 11 fundamental laws of human nature as they pertain to decision making. Great leaders recognize these fundamental laws of human nature in dealing with the stakeholders of the institutions they lead. The contemporary leader studies and examines human nature to facilitate good decision making. Understanding human nature will greatly improve school capacities for decisions to be made, implemented, and accepted.

Conceptual Framework

For leaders to make effective decisions, they must consider 11 general propositions about human nature. Consider the following when making decisions:

1. It is always about me. Whom do you consider when making decisions? Decisions in the best interest of the common good are in the best interest of institutional stakeholders.

2. People believe they are doing the right thing and doing a good job. How do you respond to this values-laden orientation? Can peoples' minds be changed when the decision is contrary to their beliefs? Inviting broad input, focusing on the common good, and maintaining objectivity can minimize this challenge.

3. Defining moments clarify and reveal relationships. Leaders who take advantage of a defining moment define what will and will not be accepted or tolerated in a professional relationship. This brings clarity to decision making.

4. People desire to leave a lasting legacy. Does your professional identity have the potential to leave a legacy? What would it be? Legacies can cloud decision making.

5. It takes a significant event to change fundamental values and beliefs. Can you change values and beliefs prior to a significant event? Effective leaders can. Decisions can be affected by rigid values and beliefs.

6. People are fundamentally good. Do you use labels such as *good, bad, smart, old,* or *exemplary* to describe your stakeholders? Labels can impose limitations and should be limited to events and actions. Challenge yourself to limit labeling.

7. The soul does not age. Do you believe this? How do you take advantage of this law to maximize contributions, productivity, and commitment?

8. People want to be liked and accepted. Do you make decisions in order to be liked or accepted? This short-term trap can marginalize the institutional good— undoing a leader's imperative.

9. People have similar basic needs. How can you fulfill basic needs such as survival, love, freedom, fun, and control, yet advance the common good? To do so is to advance decisions that are likely to gain acceptance.

10. People make mistakes. Acknowledging mistakes, accepting responsibility, and learning from them is an institutional essential. To do so will remove the need to appear flawless. This practice must be shared among all stakeholders, including the leadership.

11. People are influenced by the "law of firsts." Don't react, act instead! Is it difficult for you to consider different perspectives after hearing the first one? Leaders must consider multiple perspectives and the institutional good when making decisions.

Reflective Thinking

1. In collaborative work, there are often distinctly differing opinions shared by those who believe they are doing the right thing, for the right reasons, and for the right people. Are these really conflicting values? How do you invite diverse opinions while also converging on a final decision?

2. Glasser (1986) describes five fundamental needs that guide human behavior: survival, love, freedom, fun, and control. What other needs can you identify that are inherent to educational institutions?

3. Think of an example in which you made a visible professional mistake. How did you respond? How did you resolve the issue to your personal satisfaction and with other stakeholders? How do you respond to institutional stakeholders when they make mistakes? Is the leader's response to mistakes tied to professional risk taking? Why or why not?

7

Defining Relationships With Respect and Rapport

A house divided against itself cannot stand.

—Abraham Lincoln

In any institution and within any level of an institution, a primary function of leadership is to build capacities that allow stakeholders to reach their full potential. Leading and managing people are by far the most complex tasks in any institution. The non-people-related aspects of leadership can provide challenges, but the individuals that comprise any institution are the subjects of nearly all complex leadership challenges. If a leader has great communication and interpersonal skills (i.e., "people skills"), then the job of leading is much easier. If the leader has less than great communication and interpersonal skills, then the job can seem difficult, if not impossible.

People skills may be thought of as a leader's ability to communicate with people in ways that support healthy professional relationships. Differences of opinion may occur, and conflict is likely inevitable, but the leader possessing great people skills can minimize problems in ways that support and strengthen healthy relationships.

Great leaders must be aware of a phenomenon called the "many positive decisions versus one negative decision." This subtle phenomenon can affect leaders and their professional relationships with other people within their institutions. Leaders routinely make many decisions that positively affect people, yet when a tough decision that negatively affects these same people occurs, they are likely to forget the past favorable decisions and respond only to the unfavorable decision in isolated, "me first" ways. To minimize this, leaders must employ consistent and predictable methods of decision making (e.g., transformational decision making) and thoroughly communicate decisions to best ensure those affected understand why decisions were made. Transformational leaders must also solicit multiple sources of input from stakeholders as part of the decision-making process. This ensures that those affected by decisions had an opportunity for input and a forum to gain a fuller understanding of the criteria being considered. Additionally, dialogue through input gathering is an opportunity for leaders to communicate that decisions are based on what is in the best interest of the institution, rather than an individual. A leader who fails to solicit meaningful input and effectively communicate decision-making procedures ultimately will be placed in untenable leadership positions with institutional stakeholders when decision implementation commences.

So, how is decision-making capacity built effectively? The real key is to understand relationships and define them with respect and rapport. Understanding both of these words is critical to building and maintaining relationships with people within any institution as it relates to decision making. Although respect and rapport are simple words in form, they are complex from a leadership perspective.

Respect simply means treating others the way you want to be treated. Rapport is evidenced through the dispositions of care and concern. Professional relationships are dynamic and interactive among individuals, groups of individuals, and leaders relative to decision making. These relationships are immersed in respect and rapport. This concept is historical and universal. In education, leaders can build respect and rapport more easily with stakeholders by minimizing opportunities to single them out for either praise or criticism in front of their peers. Reprimands, discipline, and critical feedback are best handled privately rather than publicly. Other than formal opportunities (e.g., Teacher of the Year), praise in front of peers should be reserved for exceptional circumstances. Additionally, leaders must model communication that addresses a person's behavior and actions, not the person. Although basic to leadership, that idea is often forgotten.

The effective leader communicates a clear distinction between actions and behavior and people in general. This is even more critical when dealing with difficult people and challenging situations.

People want to feel that they are liked and appreciated. When a transformational leader is forced to make a tough decision, he or she has an imperative to communicate the decision rationale in collective (i.e., the common good), not individual, terms. It is absolutely essential that the leader communicate this concept effectively. Conversely, when a leader makes a decision that has derogatory effects on some institutional stakeholders, the leader must communicate that the decision was not a personal one, but rather one that was in the best interest of the institution. The leader must convey this message with *genuine* empathy, caring, and understanding. The leader, however, stands resolute in his or her resolve to do the right thing for the collective good, knowing it may have an adverse impact on some stakeholders.

Personal, positive recognition should be rewarded most often in private and not publicly in front of peers. This challenges leadership instincts. Simply stated, do not regularly single out individuals for praise in front of their peers. It is acceptable to publicly praise those not sharing peer-level responsibilities, but rarely should this be done in front of peers. Why? Many leaders can share examples of the frustration experienced when they singled someone out in an institution for praise in front of that person's peers. This can result in a performance dip by the person being singled out or a distancing of the individual from his or her peers following the public praise. Praise can inadvertently thwart leadership efforts if it is apparent that the intent was to reward the individual and to challenge others to perform to this level of praiseworthy behavior. The reason this public peer praising can create problems is typically because of an inherent need for people to belong. When singled out, an individual is distinguished from the peer group, yet the internal need to belong with this peer group usually overpowers the satisfaction of recognition or drives a greater wedge between the individual and his or her peers. Additionally, everyone believes that he or she is contributing in some way to the institution's success, and when others are not similarly recognized for praise, they can feel unappreciated and unnoticed. The institutional result can be frustration by those not selected for praise and a pressure to conform to the peer group by those singled out. Stakeholders not receiving praise may even challenge or demean the words of praise in an effort to sustain a culture of conformity. In sum, praise and criticize privately, rarely publicly.

Appropriate venues for praise include phone messages, e-mails, notes, person-to-person comments, positive evaluation comments, and other creative ways that leaders have developed for their institution. Strict adherence to a professional focus is encouraged. A professional focus includes actions, behaviors, and events. Personal comments (e.g., "You and I really connect!") should rarely be used with institutional stakeholders, but if used, they should be weighed with the utmost diligence.

Stakeholder respect is critical. A culture of respect is an essential institutional ingredient. Leaders can facilitate this by being visible, asking meaningful questions of stakeholders, listening empathically, gathering information from all levels through effective one-way and two-way communication means, and creating capacities that encourage positive and meaningful feedback about the institution. Rapport is built in similar ways, but rapport is a disposition of care and concern for institutional stakeholders. Building rapport means taking the time to get to know people on a personal-professional level without getting personal. This may seem like a competing challenge, but in reality, it makes perfect sense. Genuinely caring and asking meaningful questions of stakeholders without being overtly personal will go a long way to building rapport. Saying things like, "I've noticed you working long hours;" "I've been informed by your principal that she has been impressed with your creativity and drive, and I can't tell you how much this means to our organization;" or "How can I help ensure your success?" will all build rapport with the people in the institution.

Reprimanding an employee or student is handled differently from praise and rapport building. First, it must be done privately and with a witness present if necessary. The leader should follow policy or guidelines established by the school, district, state, and so on. Reprimanding or disciplining individuals is never easy and requires great skill on the part of the leader to maintain a professional, not personal, focus. Leaders must understand that disciplining and reprimanding an individual can change the professional relationship. Discipline and reprimands often require a different leadership style, one that is more evaluative, top-down, and supervisory. This is simply different from the collegial, enthusiastic, and collaborative leadership style that is generally representative of the transformational leader. However, all leaders will be faced with disciplining someone within their institution, and the potential impact on the professional relationship should not deter the effective leader. A transformational leader can minimize the personal nature of discipline or reprimands by using sound communication skills, keeping the meeting to a minimum time frame, and modeling transformational thinking.

Although building respect and rapport is critical to stakeholder relationships, the leader must be constantly vigilant not to let relationships dictate decision-making pedagogy. The transformational leader moves beyond the influences of individual personalities and relationships in an institution and focuses on the critical question of what is in the best interest of the institution. The transformational leader fosters good, professionally healthy relationships, while not allowing these same relationships to erode decision making to a personal level. The transformational leader understands this delicate balance.

Summary

A primary function of leadership is to build capacities that allow stakeholders to reach their full potential. This is best accomplished when a thoughtful focus is given to the necessary people skills—the leader's ability to communicate with people in ways that support healthy professional relationships. People skills should be defined by respect and rapport. Respect simply means treating others the way you want to be treated. Rapport is evidenced through the dispositions of care and concern. Respect and rapport are effective means of communicating to stakeholders that they are liked and appreciated.

Conceptual Framework

Do you have the necessary people skills to develop and communicate decisions? You can improve your people skills by considering the following:

1. Treat others the way you want to be treated.

2. Express genuine care and concern. Empathize!

3. Don't single out stakeholders in front of their peers for either praise or criticism.

4. Focus on the actions and behaviors of stakeholders. Resist generalizing.

5. Don't reduce decisions to a personal level. Always maintain a professional focus.

6. Foster respect by being visible, asking meaningful questions, listening empathically, gathering diverse opinions, and encouraging capacities for feedback.

7. Take time to get to know your stakeholders well.

Reflective Thinking

1. Should leaders build capacity for stakeholders to achieve their full potential, or should they focus on something different, such as standards of performance? What are the strengths and limitations to focusing on full potential?

2. Think of an example in which personal and professional relationships became confused. How did this limit decision making? What is your belief regarding personal and professional relationship overlap?

3. Reprimands, discipline, or simply sharing concerns as a leader with stakeholders can quickly erode to a personal, not professional, level. How do you minimize this? How do you minimize emotion when reprimanding, disciplining, or sharing concerns?

8

Entrust

The Value of Empowerment and Delegation

To be trusted is a bigger compliment than to be loved.

—George MacDonald

Historically, leaders have placed people in positions that capitalize on their gifts and talents, benefiting the common good of the institutions they represent. Leaders have routinely used the words *delegate* and *empower* to define the work they assign. Both of these words can take on similar or different meanings depending on who is assigning or what is being assigned. We believe that entrusting institutional stakeholders combines the value and worth of empowerment and delegation.

Empowering someone to oversee a project, lead peers on a task force, head a department, or carry out visions—or any similar endeavor that contributes to the growth and well-being of the institution—requires someone to serve in the leader's capacity. The stakeholders whom a leader chooses to empower must have the following characteristics: They must be aligned with the institutional vision; they must be willing to accept the assignment; they must feel confident that they can carry out the institutional directive; they must be competent to fulfill the leadership directive; they must exhibit personal and professional trustworthiness; and they must be loyal to the institutional common good.

Delegation is simply asking some person to do a task or tasks. Delegation is vital to the organization and should be considered when a leader does not have time or need to do the task, wants the task done faster than he or she can do it, has high confidence that someone else can do it faster and/or better, is gone during the required time frame to finish the task, or believes that the task should be done by someone else.

Whether empowering or delegating, effective leaders must be able to articulate the difference between what is *important* and what is *vital* within an institution. Everyone should be entrusted on an "important" level, but some tasks and assignments are different in terms of what is "vital" to the institution. The following are some guidelines for leaders to use when entrusting other people in an institution:

1. Entrust by teaching and modeling transformational decision making to all stakeholders.

2. Entrust by offering power to make decisions based on competence.

3. Entrust by offering power based on confidence.

4. Entrust to strengthen leadership.

These four guidelines are essential if the necessary empowered and delegated authority will be offered to others in carrying out the vision and mission of an institution.

Entrust by teaching and modeling transformational decision making to all stakeholders. In order for institutional stakeholders to be entrusted, they must understand the concepts of transformational decision making. Once armed with this powerful knowledge, stakeholders can communicate, articulate, and implement the strategies necessary to make great decisions. Absent this knowledge, a sound decision-making pedagogy will not be embedded in the culture of the institution. If everyone in an institution understands the concepts of sound decision making, then stakeholders will comprehend the reasoning behind decisions, and the culture will ultimately begin to reflect this comprehension. Agreement or disagreement may follow, but at least everyone will know how and why decisions were made. This allows for institutions to achieve their potential in positive ways by focusing on the common good and minimizing an individual stakeholder emphasis. If an institution is struggling for some reason, the challenges should not be from flawed decision-making pedagogy.

Entrust by offering power to make decisions based on competence. It should go without saying that leaders must share power with other institutional stakeholders to carry out important initiatives. In fact, stakeholders other than the leader are likely to be better qualified or skilled for many important tasks. Who decides the level of competence needed? The leader does so with input from a variety of sources. These sources of input may include stakeholders' experience in decision making, educational attainment or comparable experience, existing policy and guidelines, and general dispositions required for the intended purposes. Competence can be developed and competence can wane based on specific need, prior experiences, or other influencing factors. Transformational leaders will identify stakeholders who complement their skills and abilities in the best interests of the institution. Seeking competence or developing competence (i.e., skills or abilities) should be a leader's primary focus regarding personnel issues. When competence is missing or lacking in an institution, it is the leader's responsibility to build capacities for such competence as a long-range intervention and provide competence as a short-term solution.

Entrust by offering power based on confidence. Covey (1990) notes that people should be empowered based on the leader's confidence in that individual. The greater the confidence, the more empowerment is granted without direct oversight. Low confidence equates with more continual oversight, high confidence is associated with little oversight, and there are varying degrees between these two extremes. Covey views confidence as a level of competence, too. However, empowerment based on confidence must also include delegation in order to truly entrust someone. To delegate is to authorize someone to work in a limited capacity on one or more tasks. Delegation is often coupled with direct or indirect supervision. This form of leadership representation is somewhat narrower than empowerment. Delegation is focused on task accomplishment. To empower is to enable someone with the powers necessary to serve in the leader's capacity in some context of the institution. Degrees of empowerment vary, but this form of leadership focuses on serving in leadership capacities that may extend far beyond the accomplishment of a task. Thus, one can delegate without empowering, and one can empower without delegating. To truly entrust someone is to delegate tasks to someone permitted to serve in the leader's capacity.

Entrust to strengthen leadership. In order for a leader to entrust someone, those selected to be entrusted should complement the leader in ways that meet institutional needs and strengthen the institution's vision and mission. If a leader is a poor speaker, for example, then the leader must entrust someone who can fill this void. Leaders with poor communication skills must entrust someone who can do this effectively. If a leader is not an instructional leader, then, once again, the leader must entrust someone who can do this effectively. The key is to make sure that the institution's vision and mission are fulfilled. To ensure that this happens, the leader must entrust people who complement leadership challenges, making overall transformational leadership more effective and robust.

Understanding the difference between entrust, empower, and delegation. As mentioned previously, we use the word *entrust* to meld the two words *empower* and *delegate.* To entrust is a robust way of describing the value and worth of empowerment and delegation by saying, "Everyone in the institution is equally important." A person who is delegated a task must feel ownership in the institution's vision and mission just like the person who is empowered to act in a leader's capacity on a vital task. A person who has been empowered can still delegate to others or empower others in the institution. A person who has a delegated task can delegate that same task to others. To entrust is to place value and worth in all those with delegated and empowered assignments; everyone is equally important from an institutional perspective. From superintendents to secretaries, when one entrusts, one engenders ownership in the institution's welfare. This sends a strong message that everyone is equally important, whether a direct or indirect stakeholder of the institution. Are some people more vital? Yes! Is everyone equally important? Yes! Transformational leaders understand the difference and communicate this effectively to everyone in the institution. Understanding and implementing this philosophy institutionally will create a healthy and productive climate.

Leaders have known for centuries that a culture of stakeholder worth and importance is crucial, but often they have struggled with how to build this capacity for all stakeholders, regardless of role. Creating a culture that is entrusting begins the building process. Articulating the meaning behind the word *entrust* in genuine terms will build capacities for all stakeholders to feel important. Transformational leaders entrust custodians to maintain facilities, entrust secretaries to manage minute-by-minute operations, entrust teachers to ensure that student learning occurs, and entrust others to undertake significant change. All of these institutional tasks are equally important and essential to keep an institution focused on its vision and mission. However, not all tasks in an institution are equally vital. Transformational leaders entrust everyone with important tasks. Leaders must build capacities that project and articulate to stakeholders everyone's equal importance. This can be accomplished both publicly and privately. This is not the same as individual praise. Building capacities of equal importance means persuasively and emphatically projecting the importance of every single person in the institution.

An example of how this works might be a custodian for a small school. This custodian is the only custodian who works for the school during the day and is a full-time employee. The principal of the school should take the opportunity to express to this custodian how important his or her job is to the function of schooling. The leader might make comments such as, "Teaching and learning is enhanced when the facility is clean and safe. Your role ensures that." Notice that this is not the same as praising the work. It is projecting importance. The praise a leader may offer to employees in such positions can be done both publicly and privately because the custodian has no peer work group. If there were other custodians, a leader would be ill advised to single out one custodian for praise in front of other custodians. This praise should be left to more private venues. Because the custodian has no peers in terms of work assignment, others should join with the leader to project importance and offer praise regarding the efforts of the custodian when warranted. Projecting and articulating to the custodian the importance of his or her role is to help ensure institutional success.

The principal must deal slightly differently with employees in highly vital positions (e.g., technology director, curriculum director, assistant principal, department chair, and executive secretary). Consider a teacher who also serves in a department chairperson's capacity. Transformational leaders should communicate importance to all stakeholders, seeking to embed importance in the institutional culture, and the teacher-chairperson role is no exception. This dual role is also vital to the success of the school. The right person in this position can create significant teaching and learning opportunities, and the wrong person can create obstacles. From a leader's perspective, it is critical to communicate the vital nature of the teacher's chairperson capacity. Private opportunities should be considered to communicate role vitality. The leader should avoid praising role vitality in front of peers; this can create peer challenges within the institution. Some leaders may actually think that public praising raises expectations among other teachers, but actually, the opposite may be true. Competition among peer positions created by praising is often counterproductive. Not only is this master teacher (serving as a chairperson) important to the institution, he or she is also vital to the success of the school. Differences between importance and vitality regularly exist in an educational institution. A transformational leader understands the differences and finds ways to build capacities for both importance and vitality.

Summary

An effective leader realizes that all members of an institution are equally important with regard to the delegated tasks and empowerment opportunities they undertake. He or she also realizes that some roles are more vital to the success of an institution, but not more important. Great leaders communicate the concept of importance to every person in the institution and do so publicly. Communicating vitality to institution stakeholders is handled privately and not among peers. A leader understands the difference between importance and vitality. He or she projects equal importance and ensures vitality. This creates a healthy and productive climate, including a culture of worth and importance within the institution. Transformational leaders also understand that to entrust is to place equal importance on delegation and empowerment opportunities by focusing on the value and worth of each stakeholder's role.

Conceptual Framework

Delegation is requesting that someone do a task. Empowerment requires someone to act in the leader's capacity. To combine delegation and empowerment is to entrust. You can entrust others and invite meaningful decision making by considering the following guidelines:

1. Entrust by teaching and modeling transformational decision making to all stakeholders. All stakeholders need a decision-making pedagogy. How do committees in your institution currently make decisions?

2. Entrust by offering power to make decisions based on competence. Offer decision-making power to stakeholder experts! What competencies (i.e., skills or abilities) does your institution lack? Needed areas must be addressed with short-term and long-term plans.

3. Entrust by offering power based on confidence. Low confidence will require more direct oversight; high confidence will require little oversight.

4. Entrust to strengthen leadership. In other words, entrust to fulfill the institution's needs and the vision and mission. Doing so ensures that the common good remains a leadership imperative.

Reflective Thinking

1. Think of a group in which you participated that struggled to make decisions. What aspects of decision making were limitations? Was there a consistent means of making decisions? Should committees, groups, and other institutions agree on how decisions will be made? Will this enhance organizational dynamics?

2. Can a leader delegate without empowering, and vice versa? Provide an example.

3. Praising in front of peers is a common practice in educational institutions. When could this be detrimental? When could it be beneficial? Are praising and criticizing publicly equally detrimental?

9

Creating Motivating Capacities for the Common Good

To be persuasive, we must be believable. To be believable, we must be credible. To be credible, we must be truthful.

—Edward R. Murrow

Leaders of institutions constantly grapple with understanding the motivating factors that influence human behavior for the benefit of the common good. Understanding the complex nature of this challenge is the essence of creating motivating capacities. Listening to "why" and "how" questions and the resultant answer to these questions within an institution begins this journey of understanding. "Why do we have to collect data?" "Why do we need a new school facility?" "Why do we need so many rules?" "Why did I decide to teach math?" "Why must I attend the meeting?" These questions and their answers are rooted in motivation. A large body of scholarship exists on motivation. It is generally accepted that motivation is an internal state or condition that activates and energizes behavior and gives it direction (Kleinginna & Kleinginna, 1981). The sources of motivation that stir this internal state or condition are generally considered extrinsic (i.e., outside the person) or intrinsic (i.e., inside the person). Transformational decision making requires a keen focus on sources of motivation.

Extrinsic sources of motivation, such as punishments and rewards, are foundational to Glasser's (1986) notion of control issues. Glasser (1986) noted that rewards and punishments are widely used to control people. Seemingly, people may attempt to control others to get what they want by threatening, punishing, disciplining, or giving some type of reward or incentive. These external methods of motivation are often met with limited effectiveness. External motivators are limiting because motivation is an internal state or condition that is best initiated by intrinsic sources. Leaders are often misdirected in their attempts to motivate others through rewards and incentives such as salary raises and benefits. While serving an important institutional purpose, rewards and incentives are not effective sources of motivation. Externally motivating others with incentives or disincentives to meet institutional needs may glean a short-term gain, but rarely will these means be sustained as true motivators. Absent these external motivators, how does the leader create capacities for motivation?

Five key concepts are strongly aligned with transformational decision making. Consider these to be guidelines to create motivating capacities for the good of the institution. The leader must

1. Communicate transformational thinking to every member of the institution.

2. Create institutional capacities where every member is valued as equally important.

3. Create capacities that encourage input, support creativity, and honor worth.

4. Understand the fundamental laws of human nature and articulate these to the institutional membership.

5. Understand and use intrinsic and extrinsic sources of motivation.

Communicate transformational thinking to every member of the institution. As mentioned previously, it is critical that every transformational leader communicate the essence of transformational thinking. Doing so will enhance capacities for healthy motivation. If everyone in the institution understands the concepts of transformational thinking, then everyone should have a basis for understanding why decisions are made. Some may not agree with a decision, but at least they should understand the institution's mission and vision, and the importance of the common good in relation to decision making. Leaders who embed transformational thinking and decision making in the climate and culture of the schools and districts they serve are building capacities for internal and external motivation that are professionally rewarding. Stipek (1988) notes that explaining or showing the importance of something is a great source of intrinsic motivation. Importance can be reinforced extrinsically by providing clear expectations. For example, a sound vision and mission, if well-written and meaningful, communicates clear expectations and honors importance. In sum, a great leader understands the need to communicate the structure of decision making and the "what" and "why" that permeates decision making. Embedding this practice in the climate and culture of the institution can provide sources of intrinsic and extrinsic motivation that are professionally satisfying and benefit the common good.

Create institutional capacities where every member is valued as equally important. If a leader is effective in creating an environment where everyone is valued as equally important, then stakeholders will understand their role in the institution. Individuals generally want to avoid failure and achieve success. When worth and importance are lacking in an institution, individuals are likely to engage in opportunities that easily ensure success. These same individuals often hold lower expectations for success and embrace the status quo to avoid failure. Stakeholders who understand their worth and importance to the institution are more likely to accept challenging opportunities and hold higher expectations for their individual and collective success. Valued stakeholders are often the risk takers when necessary. Creating a culture and climate of importance and worth creates motivating sources that encourage stakeholders to accept challenges, establish high expectations, and strive for individual and institutional success.

Create capacities that encourage input, support creativity, and honor worth. A large body of scholarship exists that describes successful models of business in Japan. Many of these successful Japanese concepts are applicable to transformational decision making. Deming (1986), Drucker (1974), and Peters (1994) note that Japanese industrialists have created avenues to encourage input from employees on improving the company, reward creativity at every level, and honor worth in every job. Transformational leaders who embrace these practices can create powerful motivating capacities.

Suggestion cards with feedback space, collaboration meetings, discussion tables, faculty meetings, learning communities, luncheons, and retreats are a few ways that leaders can gather input from institutional members. Supporting creativity includes ways to reinforce a stakeholder's value and worth through entrusted leadership roles, provision of additional resources (e.g., time, money, supplies) necessary for success, and genuine acknowledgment of creativity. Honoring and acknowledging stakeholder worth will meet with little success unless it becomes embedded in the climate and culture of the institution. To accomplish this challenging task is to focus on it daily at all institutional levels and to ensure that it is reflected in the very vision and mission of the institution.

Understand the fundamental laws of human nature and articulate these to the institutional membership. If motivation is an internal state or condition, then understanding the fundamental laws that influence people's behavior will provide insight into what is motivating. The same fundamental laws that provide a source of motivation can also destroy motivation as it relates to the common good of the institution. Articulating, acknowledging, and communicating the laws of human behavior to institutional stakeholders will build capacities for understanding the inner self that guide behaviors and actions toward the common good. The list of 11 fundamental laws of human nature was fully described in Chapter 6.

Understand and use intrinsic and extrinsic sources of motivation. If motivation is truly an internal state, predicated on internal desire or want, then effective leaders must understand how intrinsic and extrinsic sources of motivation can affect motivating behaviors and actions. While theorists of motivation have developed extensive explanations of the internal and external factors affecting motivation, those considered to be institutionally relevant will be discussed.

Stipek (1988) describes several intrinsic actions that can be taken to increase motivation. These include, in part, explaining or demonstrating why something is important, creating and maintaining curiosity, providing variety, setting goals, and developing plans of action. Leaders who build these capacities around the institution's vision and mission will encourage internal controls that guide behaviors and actions consistent with the common good. Intrinsic means of motivating should be relied upon to embed long-term sources of institutional motivation in the climate and culture.

Extrinsic means of motivating can be powerful for short durations but should not supplant the importance of an intrinsic focus. Stipek

(1988) suggests that extrinsic sources of motivation should include clear expectations, corrective feedback, and valuable rewards (e.g., valuable resources such as time, competitive salaries and benefits, and supplies and materials).

Establishing clear expectations through goal setting is particularly noteworthy. Goals often range from simple to complex, straightforward to ambiguous, and measurable to not measurable. In spite of the broad range, effective goals should provoke meaningful "how" and "why" questions. These questions enjoin individual motivation and the common good in ways that benefit the institution. Setting clear expectations through goal setting is an effective source of motivation that ultimately benefits the institution.

Summary

Understanding the motivating factors that influence human behavior will greatly benefit the common good. Listening to "why" and "how" questions and the resultant answer to these questions is tantamount to building motivational capacity. Additionally, leaders can nurture motivating capacities by communicating transformational thinking to every member of the institution; ensuring that every stakeholder is valued as equally important; encouraging input, supporting creativity, and honoring worth; understanding the fundamental laws of human nature and articulating these to the institutional membership; and understanding and using intrinsic and extrinsic sources of motivation.

Conceptual Framework

Consider the following to be guidelines to creating motivating capacities for the common good of the institution.

1. Communicate transformational thinking to every member of the institution. What does this have to do with motivation? Communicating improves the capacity to understand why decisions are made. Vision, mission, and the common good are understood as a basis for decision making. Decision making becomes predictable—a motivating capacity.

2. Create institutional capacities where every member is valued as equally important. This helps stakeholders understand their real roles and responsibilities in the institution. This, in turn, serves to strengthen worth and importance—a source of motivation.

Do you work most effectively when your roles and responsibilities are clearly defined?

3. Create capacities that encourage input, support creativity, and honor worth. These must be embedded in the culture of the institution in order to sustain themselves as motivating capacities.

4. Understand the 11 fundamental laws of human nature, and articulate these to the institutional membership. They will provide insight into what is motivating.

5. Understand and use intrinsic and extrinsic sources of motivation. Build capacity for these sources around the institution's vision and mission to guide behaviors and actions consistent with the common good. Intrinsic sources include, in part, explaining or demonstrating why something is important, creating and maintaining curiosity, providing variety, setting goals, and developing plans of action. Extrinsic sources include, in part, valuable rewards (e.g., time, competitive salaries and benefits, and supplies and materials); clear expectations; and corrective feedback (Stipek, 1988). Can you think of others?

Reflective Thinking

1. Provide examples of several "why" and "how" questions that can reveal sources of motivation.

2. We provided representative sources of intrinsic and extrinsic motivation. What other sources exist in your institution?

3. Encouraging and being responsive to input from stakeholders both serve as a genuine source of motivation. Brainstorm examples of ways in which you solicit feedback. How were you responsive to the feedback?

10

The Influence
of Capitalism on
Decision Making

*Competition brings out the best in products and the
worst in people.*

—David Sarnoff

Free-market capitalism with minimal government intervention is an American ideology (Cooper, Fusarelli, & Randall, 2004) immersed in competition (Bast & Walberg, 2003). In fact, anyone suggesting alternatives is quickly exiled to the "margins of mainstream discourse" (Bosso, 1994, p. 185). This poses significant challenges for educational institutions and their leaders, and necessitates a thorough understanding of the significant capitalistic concepts that go unnoticed or are misunderstood and misapplied in education. Furthermore, the transformational leader must build capacities to understand and acknowledge contemporary capitalism in order to lead educational institutions effectively. In relation to for-profit capitalism, leaders have made decisions based largely on factors such as gross domestic product, economies, distribution, products, services, profits, trends, change, improvement, and market forces. But rarely is capitalism studied, understood, and used appropriately in not-for-profit institutions, although it has a powerful and unique influence on nonprofit institutions such as education. By understanding how two distinct sectors (i.e., for-profit and not-for-profit) differ fundamentally, leaders of educational institutions can make informed decisions that affect teaching and learning in profound ways.

Edward Deming is well known in many leadership circles for introducing the Japanese philosophy of industry and production to America. Deming's ideas were widely embraced by the for-profit sector in hopes of prospering, and his message of quality ushered in a national revolution of new production and service concepts during the 1980s. This same philosophy quickly spilled over into areas where it did not easily fit. Yet few leaders challenged the notions that had been so widely embraced. The Japanese model seemed to make perfect sense, and many for-profit and not-for-profit institutions adopted it with enthusiasm.

As many in the for-profit sector discovered that wholesale adoption and implementation of someone else's model did not meet with overwhelming success, educational institutions also realized that imitating others, or adopting a list-logic approach (Barth, 1990) to teaching and learning, rarely met with success. Transformational leaders know that defensive and spontaneous reactions, compliance without buy-in, and strict adherence to a model rarely solve any problem. Nor will imitation and copying the successes of others solve complex educational challenges. Institutions, by their very nature, can problem-solve adequately through their own internal means of improvement. By focusing on the cooperation and collaboration characteristics that are unique to an institution's culture, internal solutions will prove to be the only meaningful and long-term answer for genuine improvement of any kind.

Capitalism is alive and well in the world. It is an invisible market force that has generated an awesome economy. Capitalism has created wealth and happiness in this country, the likes of which have never been duplicated in the annals of time. Capitalism has a track record of proven success around the world, but an expanded understanding must be addressed to fully understand the power behind this awesome and comprehensive system (Bast & Walberg, 2003). Although capitalism is an accepted, if not hard-to-define, phenomenon, it is, nevertheless, a challenging economic principle when it comes to not-for-profit institutions. Understanding capitalism as it relates to not-for-profit institutions will help the contemporary educational leader in making transformational decisions. Understanding not-for-profit institutions economically gives the reader an expanded understanding of capitalism.

Product and service capitalism is driven by invisible market forces and serves as the backbone of the free enterprise system in this country. Basic tenets of for-profit capitalism involve the generally accepted practices of free enterprise—allowing the marketplace to dictate personnel, prices, costs, quantity, quality, production parameters, controls, and growth. Competition is a key concept in understanding traditional product and service capitalism. Competition drives products and services in terms of quantity and quality. Prices, wages, product viability, success, failure, and growth are all left to the market forces. Competition underscores these market forces. For-profit entities must be competitive in order to sell their products and services to the consumer. If they do not compete, they cannot survive. Many economists would say, "Leave the capitalistic system alone and the economy will flourish and prosper." Even amidst a healthy economy, companies that do not compete will either improve or disappear. This system has proven highly effective in the production- and service-oriented for-profit sector. Simply put, it works! And competition is at the very heart and soul of for-profit economics.

As effective as competition capitalism is in for-profit economics, the same cannot be said of not-for-profit educational institutions. Educational institutions must be driven by cooperation, not competition, in order to be effective. Clear distinctions between for-profit and not-for-profit institutions exist, making the application of competitive capitalism difficult for educational institutions. Educational institutions do not choose the students they serve, but rather serve *all* children; they are governed by elected or appointed officials selected outside the control of the institution itself and are immersed in democracy and federalism; they cannot move the institution's location easily or control other demographic characteristics; they cannot always control educational inputs, such as fiscal issues; they are controlled by output measures such as equity, adequacy, and achievement; they cannot naturally grow without outside influence; and they usually will not disappear if they are unproductive. These distinctions are not all-inclusive, but assist in building a framework that distinguishes educational institutions.

The for-profit and not-for-profit sectors are also distinguished on the grounds of people, products, and services. Educational institutions exist for students (i.e., a people orientation), with products and services providing the tools to deliver an education. The for-profit sector focuses on products and services as means to reach their customers (i.e. a product and service orientation). Products and services are not people. People make products or provide services, but people are not products or services. It is on these grounds that leaders must reflect on their views of competition and cooperation. Products and services generally can be controlled as leaders select, improve, eliminate, increase, decrease, change, and charge more or less for products or services. Many more words could be used to describe the actions of a leader regarding products and services. Some of the same words can describe the actions of an educational leader with regard to people, but many cannot. Simply stated, people are distinctly different from products and services. It is true that people are capable of producing products and services, but the people themselves cannot be altered, improved, or manipulated like a product or service. This belief is foundational to understanding how the two institutional sectors differ. Products and services flourish in a capitalistic economy underscored by competition. People (i.e., educational stakeholders) flourish when educational institutions are underscored by cooperation.

Competition is a natural human disposition, and so is cooperation. Both competition and cooperation are healthy means of achieving excellence. Competition and cooperation can be readily found in the for-profit and not-for-profit sectors. However, as leaders reflect on the inherent differences in each sector, it becomes readily apparent that competition and cooperation are often competing dimensions. In other words, to gain ground cooperatively means to minimize competition, and likewise, to become competitive means to minimize cooperation. This does not mean that both (i.e., cooperation and competition) cannot coexist in each sector. They do! However, both cannot be equally important, equally embedded in the culture, and equally reflected in the mission and vision of the institution. For educational institutions, focusing on cooperation fosters meaningful improvement and growth, but at the expense of a competitive environment. To maximize competition at the expense of cooperation can be an obstacle to the improvement process in educational institutions by reducing teaching and learning to a win-lose proposition. In an *all-student* orientation, competition simply cannot level an educational playing field immersed in equity and adequacy. Educational environments are often defined on the grounds of equality (i.e., sameness), equity (i.e., fairness), and adequacy (i.e., sufficiency). The assumption that these important driving forces of education can be achieved is premised on the fact that educational cultures are defined by cooperation. Would equality, equity, and adequacy survive in a competitive environment? It is doubtful.

People can exhibit competitive behaviors when the need arises. For example, survival and basic needs can generate a high degree of competitiveness. These can include, among others, the need for nourishment, sleep, affiliation, and job employment. The basic needs and survival of business, industry, and other for-profit stakeholders who must endure and thrive through their products and services give rise to the same competitive tendencies individuals often exhibit. In this type of competitive environment, some will survive, some will thrive, and many will fail. However, competition in not-for-profit educational institutions discourages meaningful growth, the sharing of successes, and cooperation, and it generally builds a cocoon of "win-lose" around the institution in an effort to remain competitive. This cocoon serves to perpetuate a climate that can be physically and mentally draining as winning drives decision making and losing is discouraged. Education can never afford to simply win or lose!

Not-for-profit educational institutions do not function effectively in a competitive environment. Providing an education for *all* students is simply not possible in a competitive environment. A free and appropriate education cannot be had unless cooperation and collaboration permeate the institution. When institutions cooperate internally and externally, continuous and persistent improvement can be realized for *all* students. Cooperation minimizes failure in educational institutions and encourages risk and growth for the common good.

Educational institutions flourish and improve when encouraged to cooperate instead of compete. Imagine schools cooperating and collaborating to share ideas and programs; imagine schools working cooperatively to attract educators, share services, create overlapping facilities, and work together persistently for the betterment of all students; imagine school districts cooperating to pool resources, services, and programs. Many schools and districts are already experiencing these shared benefits to some extent, but competition serves to threaten cooperative efforts and negate the rewards of such arrangements.

Leaders of the for-profit sector should understand and embrace the principles of competition. Leaders of not-for-profit educational institutions should understand that cooperation must be nurtured among and between schools and districts to create a healthy environment of sustained improvement and success. Cooperation must overshadow competitive tendencies in education. Educational leaders must resist the urge to apply competitive practices to their institutions. Doing so breeds a competitive climate and culture that is unhealthy, and at times unethical. For example, a building principal may overemphasize standardized test scores and do so in a competitive way. The clear message to school stakeholders is, "We must win and have the highest scores." When an institution's leader communicates a win-lose message, school stakeholders might respond to this unrealistic expectation by using unethical means to win. This might include making unapproved copies of standardized tests from which to teach and learn, teaching to the test rather than from the curriculum, and altering standardized tests. Simply stated, school and district improvement capacities are nurtured in a cooperative environment, not a competitive one.

Today's educational institutions are experiencing greater external influences. State and federal policies, for example, have raised accountability standards and shifted control to ensure effective teaching and learning. Meeting these rigorous expectations in a culture of competition will surely spell failure. Transformational leaders are well advised to create cooperative capacities that allow school stakeholders to be held to high expectations in a nonthreatening environment. To do otherwise is educationally destructive.

Public schools and the education they provide are better than ever before. America's public schools now have an exceedingly high literacy rate (Krashen, 1993). Literacy, defined simply as the ability to read and write at a basic level, has been steadily rising in the United States for the past 100 years (Stedman & Kaestle, 1987). Even the "long-term prognosis for school-business partnerships is promising" (Gray, 2000, p. 633). Beyond K–12 schooling, America's higher education system is considered by many other nations as "the envy of the world" (Reindl, 2004). So, what is the crisis? There is no crisis; there are only challenges.

Then what is the answer? Build capacities for cooperation that strengthen the institution's vision and mission, and improvement will naturally follow. Schools want to improve just as people do. Each school and district is unique and requires different capacities. Great transformational leaders recognize this and do not force one-size-fits-all approaches to improvement.

External mandates, standards, and student achievement policies should not be interpreted as raising *all* students to the same performance level. Sameness should not be confused with fairness and sufficiency. Our world was not intended to function with everyone being the same. Not everyone will choose to go to college, and not everyone will want to be a doctor, attorney, or teacher. Competition is more likely to accomplish educational sameness, not educational fairness or sufficiency. A few years ago, for example, the for-profit competitive sector experienced a spectacular collapse of dot-coms with few survivors (Cottrill, 2002; Maiello, 2002), and business investments, especially in technology equipment, plunged (Ip, 2002). This is accepted in a capitalistic society, but if schools had this failure rate, a national crisis would surely ensue.

Relying on competition to drive institutional improvement in education is destructive and creates an environment where improvement is even harder to attain because failure is feared, winning underscores teaching and learning, and sameness becomes more important than fairness or sufficiency. Cooperation minimizes failure in educational institutions by encouraging risk and growth for the common good.

Summary

Competition is a key concept in understanding traditional product and service capitalism. Competition drives products and services in terms of quantity and quality. Prices, wages, product viability, success, failure, and growth are all left to the market forces. Competition underscores these market forces. For-profit entities must be competitive in order to sell their products and services to the consumer. If they do not compete, they cannot survive. The same cannot be said of not-for-profit educational institutions. Educational institutions must be driven by cooperation, not competition, in order to be effective. Clear distinctions between for-profit and not-for-profit institutions exist, making the application of competitive capitalism difficult for educational institutions. Leaders of not-for-profit educational institutions should understand that cooperation must be nurtured among and between schools and districts to create a healthy environment of sustained improvement and success. Cooperation must overshadow competitive tendencies in education. Transformational leaders must resist the urge to apply competitive practices to their institutions. Doing so breeds a competitive climate and culture that are unhealthy and, at times, unethical.

Conceptual Framework

Do capitalistic product and service market forces influence your decision making? Educational leaders must be able to distinguish between the tenets of for-profit, capitalistic institutions and not-for-profit, educational institutions if informed decisions are to be made.

1. Focus on cooperation and collaboration, and minimize competition, when making decisions.

2. Avoid one-size-fits-all approaches to provide decisions for complex educational issues. Institutions have the internal means

to solve problems and make decisions. Doing so builds buy-in capacity and encourages sustained improvement and success.

Reflective Thinking

1. Can schools successfully adopt one-size-fits-all approaches to school improvement? Why or why not? Give examples in practice that have worked and failed.

2. To what extent is competition part of your climate or culture? Is competition healthy in educational institutions?

3. How has the for-profit sector (e.g., business and industry) influenced your educational institution? Is the influence healthy or unhealthy?

11

Refining and Rethinking Change in Education

Absolutely everything moves forward.

—Carl Sagan

A persistent phenomenon that permeates the educational landscape is *change.* For several decades, the pace of change in schools has quickened, having an indelible effect on climate, culture, and decision making. Change can erode sound decision-making pedagogy when it strays from the original mission and vision of the institution and is heavily influenced externally.

Leaders have generally accepted that change is good, natural, inevitable, and essential to the health and well-being of educational institutions. Many leaders are change advocates, embedding it in the culture of the institution. In fact, it is not unusual to see leaders adopting aggressive change agendas, believing it to be the only way to not disappear from the educational landscape. However, change beliefs can be effective in some instances while being damaging or even fatal in other instances.

The profound influence of a profit-driven value structure, especially as it relates to change, necessitates well-articulated decision making. Drucker (1990) notes in his book *Managing the Non-Profit Organization* that, unlike the for-profit sector, not-for-profit leaders tend to make fewer decisions, are less likely to make risky decisions, attend lots of meetings, and tend to avoid difficult decisions that might harm people. He further notes that leaders in the nonprofit sector might incidentally feed a problem and overlook opportunities to resolve problems because they lack the will to act decisively. These leadership challenges are often deeply embedded in the educational institution's culture, which encourages shared decision making, little risk, and students as the first and foremost decision imperative. These challenges compel the transformational leader to embrace a consistent and sound decision-making pedagogy.

The previous chapter was dedicated to the market value of competition and the competing value of cooperation. Similarly, the market value of change, a lucid and necessary component found in capitalism, competes with educational institutions' tight and often tenacious culture.

Capitalistic values promote a for-profit sector that is competitive and adaptable to change. For-profit institutions whose value structure is not loosely coupled enough to change are less likely to provide competitive products or services. Change in profit-seeking institutions is good and necessary to prosper. Companies that do not change or improve their product or service may disappear from the economic landscape. Viewing change through the for-profit lens validates its importance and essential capitalistic contributions. However, the vision and mission of the educational institution is not focused on products or services, and change does not always apply universally to these unique institutions. Change has a very different value orientation when viewed through an educational lens.

Educational institutions often operate under the pretense of change. Because change underpins capitalism and is a foundational market value, the language of change frequently permeates educational rhetoric and discourse in an effort to forge a link to this widely held American value. Educational leaders who frequently speak the language of change not only resonate with those believing in this for-profit value, but also communicate an inverse message to those they serve that not advocating change is undemocratic. And although this may influence the *received* culture (Goodwyn, 1978), or what is considered legitimate and acceptable, the *actual* culture in educational institutions will likely continue to resist change.

It could be argued that the greatest change not naturally occurring in educational institutions includes technology and other capital improvements. Remove computers, technological innovations, and capital improvements such as building renovations from educational change agendas, and it is challenging to identify meaningful change that has significantly altered educational institutions other than by natural occurrence. Prestine and McGreal (1997) note that teachers not believing in the need for change will not make it part of their classroom repertoire. This begs the question of why so many educational leaders continually advocate change, especially change that is externally motivated, in the institutions they serve when it may not be warranted, necessary, or effective.

One could argue that instructional methodologies have changed, curriculum has changed, and leadership has changed, but any real and meaningful changes have naturally occurred as a result of internal institutional influences, not external forces. Examples of meaningful internal changes might include developing healthier school climates and cultures, valuing diversity, believing that all students really can learn, and strengthening school-community relations. It is important to remember that educational institutions exist at multiple levels (i.e., federal, state, local). So, even in the absence of free-market forces, legitimate educational forces (e.g., state Department of Education, federal Department of Education) that are leveraging change are often viewed as external stakeholders and are rejected at differing levels. The recent federal mandates of the No Child Left Behind Act serve as an excellent example of legitimate leveraging that must be considered but is frequently rejected. At best, change should be initiated and should occur at the level where the need naturally exists. This would imply less external leveraging and more partnerships among educational institutional levels (Wilson & Rossman, 1993). Yet educational institutions continue to hold in a pattern of external change expectations influenced by consequences for failure and rewards for success rather than partnership opportunities that are win-win.

A common misconception is that leaders can change people. Many would argue that it is impossible to change a person. Only individuals can truly change themselves, not others. This implies that effective leaders build capacities within an institution for people to change. These capacities might include defining a compelling need, advocating risk-taking, providing resources and professional development, establishing realistic goals, and establishing a slow pace for change. Building these capacities and others will allow educational stakeholders to change themselves, ensuring meaningful and sustained change that benefits the institution.

Urging rapid and reformation-laden change, many statespeople, proprietary think tanks, business leaders, and organized advocacies such as chambers of commerce have all tried unsuccessfully to apply free-market values to educational institutions, touting students as products and learning as a service. This assumes measured, algorithmic input and output variables. However, teaching and learning are not that simple. Students are not products, and teaching is not a free-market, competitive service. For-profit attempts to quantify revenue inputs as they directly relate to learning outputs will continue to prove confounding. Transformational leaders who embrace free-market influences for education stand to change the future of American society and the individuals who constitute society in devastating ways.

Learning is a natural phenomenon influenced by physical, biological, and environmental factors. For example, it is possible to improve the physical nature of a person, limited only by his or her potential for change. For example, a person running the 100-meter dash can improve his or her time by a given amount, but not every person can run this dash under 10 seconds. Many athletes have the potential to improve their vertical jump, but most cannot dunk the basketball; it is simply not possible. Likewise, no amount of legislation, consequences, or implementation mandates will ever allow some students to meet unrealistic learning expectations regardless of change efforts. This is not to say that leaders should accept failure, incompetence, mediocrity, minimal effort, excuses, or a lack of readiness. It simply means that institutional leaders must be cognizant of change that is not realistic and imposes artificial standards that uniformly fit everyone (i.e., one size fits all). Individuals are not the same, they never will be the same, and they should never be the same. No amount of change can alter this fact.

The key to transformational leadership is to build capacities that allow educational stakeholders to reach their change potential for improvement and growth. Decision making is strongly aligned with building capacity. Both will flow naturally if they focus on the vision and mission of the institution. Absent that focus, external forces can erode capacity and decision making. To improve education is to allow the naturalness of institutional thinking and decision making to be embraced by the enterprise.

When the breadth of institutional levels in education is considered from the student and teacher level through the federal level, cooperative partnerships have the change potential for public education to improve and grow in ways never imagined. Imagine the power of improvement that could be achieved by encouraging teams of schools to partner on teaching and learning challenges, pool resources, share training, discuss students of similar need, and initiate change based on the vision and mission of the institution. Schools will improve naturally, although not in every area every year. Each year, the students change, the faculty changes, and leadership may change, but the institution will remain. Mandating unrealistic outcomes, imposing external restrictions, scripting standards that narrowly define what students should know, and enacting high-stakes consequences or menial rewards violates the logical constructs for school improvement and does nothing to encourage meaningful change.

Summary

Capitalism is the greatest economic system the world has ever known. Adam Smith's concepts were genius. However, for educational institutions to prosper and grow, the for-profit values of competition and externally influenced change must be minimized in favor of more effective change alternatives. A focus on cooperation can encourage partnerships among the varying levels of educational institutions. Partnerships will serve as a more meaningful catalyst for inside-out change, rather than external change agendas. Beyond the pedagogical constructs called Transformational Laws that were discussed in Chapter 2, effective leaders can build internal change capacities that support the institution's vision and mission by considering the following: Develop compelling needs when change is necessary, encourage risk-taking, reallocate resources to support change initiatives, provide professional development and training, establish clear goals for change, and recognize the slow pace that meaningful change often requires.

Conceptual Framework

The educational landscape is rich with change. However, meaningful change must focus on the mission, the vision, and the common good.

1. Assess your own change capacity. Are you a change advocate? If so, you can exhaust stakeholders if the culture is not adaptable to change. Change capacity begins with a commitment to shared decision making within the institution.

2. Discuss change issues, both internal and external to the institution, with stakeholders. Which change issues are necessary to address, meaningful, aligned with institutional work, and likely to be supported and sustained? The answers, in part, determine your change agenda.

3. Build capacities within your building for stakeholders to change. Leaders do not change stakeholders—stakeholders change themselves. Focus on resources, professional development, risk-taking, and clearly defined change issues.

4. Change takes time. Fast-paced change often is not sustained in the institution, especially if stakeholders don't believe in the change. Are you willing to advocate for change, understanding that meaningful change takes time? To do so is to build change capacity.

Reflective Thinking

1. How would you describe your educational institution's capacity for change (e.g., resistant or adaptable)? What strategies do you use to address change issues? How does your institution's ability to change influence your decision making?

2. Do collaborative cultures resist or invite change? What factors support your position?

3. Describe a change that failed and a change that was embraced and sustained. What factors influenced these changes?

12

Facing the Challenges of Leadership

The future belongs to those who believe in the beauty of their dreams.

—Eleanor Roosevelt

The leader of any institution, regardless of position, will encounter challenges and make decisions that are judged by others as unfavorable. Challenging decisions cannot be avoided, but avoiding the pitfalls of leadership can enhance acceptance of these difficult decisions. For example, a school principal may make a series of student discipline decisions that appear to be inconsistent to teachers. A superintendent who suggests a tax raise as necessary to meet educational needs might be judged as having made an unfavorable decision by board members staunchly opposed to tax increases. Effective leaders minimize the negative impact of challenging decisions by constantly strengthening the moral and ethical dimensions of their leadership and avoiding five destructive pitfalls that erode trust.

The first destructive pitfall is making decisions that are in the leader's self-interest or in the self-interest of others. Selfish interests in decision making could involve family members, fellow workers, significant others, and groups that exert pressure to further their advocacy interests. These interests might include promises, perks, memberships, votes, affiliations, or simply the avoidance of negative consequences. How does one make decisions that may adversely affect someone close to him or her? And how does one make decisions when surrounded by difficult circumstances? The answer is transformational decision making through strong moral and ethical leadership. Leaders armed with transformational decision-making knowledge, coupled with the conviction to act morally and ethically, will ultimately make outstanding decisions that eventually lead to highly functioning institutions. Leading from a moral and ethical paradigm is the sign of a professionally mature leader. A mature leader knows that decision making is often clouded with competing issues, but strives to keep decisions transparent and easily understood. Focusing on the common good of the institution and its vision and mission is tantamount to leadership success.

Decisions that are subjective rather than objective can taint good leadership and serve as a second destructive pitfall. Decision making can be fraught with emotion and motivations that impede effective leadership when research, valid and reliable data, and objective input from multiple sources are not considered. These unhealthy influences encourage the leader's use of opinion or gut feeling and do not allow for the time necessary to make unbiased decisions. Furthermore, transformational leaders who make subjective decisions model a destructive behavior for other institutional stakeholders. Consider the teacher who is asked what evidence exists for the instructional methodology used, and the response is, "I know in my heart this is best for kids." Would an effective leader accept this answer as the sole rationale? No! Nor should leaders guide their decisions with subjective rationales.

Decisions that are illegal, the third destructive pitfall, can never be supported. Great leaders have the conviction to act legally at all times. Anything less is not acceptable. The definition of what is or is not legal lies somewhere along a continuum between right and wrong. Leaders whose moral compass guides them make decisions that never give the appearance of impropriety and are generally considered right. In our federalist system of school governance, transformational leaders are an arm of the government and as such have an obligation to ensure that the public's educational interests are satisfied. The leader who takes one postage stamp from the educational institution to mail a personal letter has violated this interest. Although taking one postage stamp may seem trivial, imagine how it would be interpreted if run as a headline and cover story in your local paper. Leaders can tap their moral compass by asking how a particular decision will be interpreted by the public if given a headline and run as a cover story in the local paper. If you do not like the answer to this question, it may have immoral underpinnings.

In an era of high-stakes accountability (e.g., No Child Left Behind), dwindling resources amidst a faltering economy, increased time demands, and changing roles, stress underscores transformational leadership and serves as a fourth destructive pitfall. Simply stated, public education is a fertile environment for stress. Responses to these stressors include high rates of job turnover; earlier retirements; mental and physical illnesses, including death; addictions; and a paucity of candidates to fill vacant positions. Given the dynamic and complex work environment of transformational leaders, stress cannot be avoided. Therefore, it must be acknowledged and understood if its effects are to be reduced and minimized.

Martin and Willower (1981) found that most administrators perceived their work environment as routine rather than stressful, even when faced with excessive workloads and unrealistic time commitments. Milstein and Farkas (1988) note that stress may be deflected by turning to sources other than the job for needs fulfillment. This could include families, friends, supportive groups and communities, and hobbies. Thus, detachment from work may help negate job-related stress. However, when the challenging work environment is no longer routine, or when needs fulfillment is destructive (e.g., alcohol abuse or gambling), stress erodes effective leadership. Leaders must understand the highly personal nature of responding to stress (i.e., what is stressful to one may not be to another) and find healthy, productive ways to deal with stress.

The fifth of the destructive pitfalls is probably the hardest to define. It is often referred to by institutional stakeholders as the ineffectiveness of the leader. This perceived ineffectiveness comes from any one of a number of areas that are vital to the operation of an institution. Ineffectiveness in some areas (e.g., the effort to be visible in the community) may not adversely affect the institution, yet other ineffective qualities (e.g., providing instructional leadership) can have a profoundly negative impact on an institution. Most leaders cannot be wholly effective in all areas. However, great leaders understand their own inadequacies and find ways to build capacities in these challenge areas. For example, a superintendent may lack the knowledge and talents necessary to build an annual budget. The wise leader would rely on someone else's fiscal strengths to build the budget. Only the leader who does not recognize his or her fiscal weaknesses and builds budgets in spite of them is likely to be deemed fiscally ineffective by others. The answer to dealing with perceived ineffectiveness is for the leader to self-assess inadequacies and identify others who can strengthen these shortcomings. This does not imply that leaders should hide their shortcomings, but rather deal with them in positive ways. This act of humility will strengthen the leader and the institution.

Summary

The leader of any institution, regardless of position, will encounter challenges and make decisions that are judged by others as unfavorable. Avoiding the five pitfalls of leadership (i.e., making decisions that are in the leader's self-interest or in the self-interest of others; making decisions that are subjective rather than objective; making decisions that are illegal; not finding healthy, productive ways to deal with the stress of decision making; and leader ineffectiveness) can enhance acceptance of these difficult decisions.

Conceptual Framework

Leaders can minimize the impact of difficult decisions by strengthening stakeholder trust through the moral and ethical dimensions of leadership. Five considerations, although alluded to in earlier chapters, are so pervasive and persistent that they warrant exclusive consideration.

1. Do you make decisions that are in your self-interest or in the self-interest of others? In resisting this temptation, decisions are transparent and easily understood.

2. Do you make decisions that are subjective rather than objective? Doing so relies on emotions, assumptions, and potentially harmful motivations. Subjective decisions often lack diverse perspectives and the time needed for objectivity.

3. Do you make decisions that are illegal, believing that rules are made to be broken? You must protect the public's educational interests and allow your moral and ethical compass to guide you. Imagine each of your decisions being featured as the local paper's cover story. Would the headlines be favorable, supporting the legal perspectives of your educational decision?

4. Do you find healthy, productive ways to deal with the stress of decision making? What do you turn to for needs fulfillment? Are you able to detach from work the job-related stress of difficult decisions?

5. Can you articulate your own ineffectiveness as a leader? How you do build capacities that support these ineffective qualities? To do so is to strengthen decision making.

Reflective Thinking

1. What moral or ethical imperatives guide your leadership? Describe an example in practice of each moral or ethical consideration.

2. What is your greatest challenge area in leadership? How do you strengthen it?

3. What are your greatest job-related stressors? How do you deflect (i.e., minimize or negate) them? Does stress influence your decision making?

13

Leadership for the Common Good

The Essential Imperative

We are made wise not by the recollection of our past, but the responsibility for our future.

—George Bernard Shaw

The mission of this book is to give leaders the confidence and empowerment to act decisively with a sound decision-making pedagogy—transformational decision making. School leaders who practice the pedagogy of transformational decision making will find themselves leading in profoundly positive and meaningful ways. Institutional stakeholders will also benefit as the vision, mission, and overall common good permeate decisions.

This book was not designed to tell leaders what decisions to make, but rather how to make decisions by providing a framework of sound decision making. It would be impossible to provide school leaders with a template that considers all the unique contexts of decision making. However, if leaders are of sound mind, understand human nature, are uninfluenced by obstacles, value a common vision and mission, practice respect and rapport, entrust others, understand motivation, and have a keen awareness of the contemporary capitalistic values influencing education, then the leader is free to simply ask the question, "What is in the best interest of the institution I lead?" To determine the outcome of this question requires clear and transparent thinking on the part of any leader. Some leaders act with transformational thinking, and this book simply affirms a proven pedagogy. Other leaders may find themselves focused on other aspects of the complex challenges of education, paying little attention to a decision-making pedagogy. We hope that this book profoundly affects the decision-making abilities of all educational leaders. Transformational decision making will better ensure successful leadership.

The first step toward transformational thinking is for the leader to resolve the agony of worrying about how the decision will affect stakeholders inside or outside the institution. Expending energy on worry simply muddies the water of sound decision making and detracts from leadership effectiveness. The leader must have the confidence to know that when leadership is guided by a meaningful vision and mission, what is best for the institution is best for the collective good. This will generally translate to individual stakeholder good. This can be a challenging concept to grasp because an institution does not physically exist. An institution cannot compliment or say thanks to a leader. So, the leader is making a decision in the best interest of something that cannot talk, give feedback, or be grateful for the decisions that help the institution. On the other hand, people affected by the decisions of leaders can share concerns, compliments, and an array of positive and negative feedback. The decisions made by leaders that negatively affect people create pressures and strains that result in undesirable decision making at times. These pressures and strains can become so great that what is best for the institution is no longer a guiding light for decision making.

Leadership can be lonely absent collegial and collaborative peer networks and other feedback opportunities. Leadership feedback is often wrought with negative, emotional messages. If this is the only kind of feedback a leader receives, confidence in focusing on the vision, mission, and common good can wane. To combat this challenge, a constant focus on moral leadership must be practiced to move decision making beyond limited feedback to the greater institutional good. It is when leaders consistently make decisions in the best interest of individuals rather than the institutions they lead that confusion reigns and the institution is placed in jeopardy. When institutions are placed in peril, the concept of collective good begins to erode and systemic breakdown commences. Loneliness can also be combated through collegial and collaborative peer networks that offer opportunities to maintain a focus on the common good by assessing decisions and their impact among others making similar decisions.

Leaders know that decisions may adversely affect people, creating a sense of loneliness at the top, increasing professional stress, and eroding longevity and job security. This challenges any decision-making model. How does one get leaders to move beyond this burdensome hurdle? The answer lies in making a decisive and persistent choice to implement transformational decision making at all times, communicating this theory of leadership decision making to everyone in the institution. If this is done properly and universally, the leader can make decisions with a clear conscience and with the resolve that the decision was appropriate. Those challenging decisions the most are likely viewing the decisions through the lens of the first fundamental law of human nature . . . it is always about me. It does not make them bad people; they simply want what is best for themselves. These people may have no real interest in the institution other than a job or position. The effective leader understands that time is a critical decision-making element. Transformational decisions may take time, which is often subject to criticism from those wanting simple solutions to complex issues, but transformational decisions are more meaningful and aligned with the common good.

Great leadership at any level of an institution requires a strong personal resolve, a persistent resilience to criticism, a powerful conviction of purpose, and a clear conscience when making decisions. The following are three transformational considerations that permeate effective leadership.

1. Leaders should strive to ensure success, but these same leaders should never be fearful of allowing stakeholders to grow, in part, by failing. Everyone has a right to fail or succeed. Leaders have a moral obligation to ensure that teaching and learning reaches its full potential, and failure may be a part of this process. Decisions should be made that focus on achieving vision and mission potential, not just success or failure, and not simply winning or losing.

2. Discipline is in the best interest of the institution. Discipline is different from punishment and threats, which should never be accepted in schools. When schools implement discipline procedures to ensure an appropriate learning environment, they are actually defining acceptable behaviors for the common

good, encouraging self-control, and communicating clear expectations. Disciplinary procedures and rules should be developed at each institutional level. Oversight from other interdependent institutions may be necessary but should occur in a limited capacity to encourage decision making at the lowest level.

3. District-level decisions should center on district-level impact, just as building-level decisions should focus on building-level impact. In other words, at each institutional level, the vision and mission should drive decision making. Day-to-day decisions should be left to the lowest level of appropriate leadership with other institutional leaders serving as resource providers, not decision makers. Higher-level leadership then serves in a support role to assist, recommend, and give objective information. Why? Because institutional decisions should be maintained at the lowest level where the vision, mission, and common good have the greatest meaning and value. It is important for all leaders to understand that the true meaning and value of an institution's vision, mission, and common good are profoundly different among differing institutional levels.

Armed with the power of transformational thinking and decision making, you now garner the knowledge to effectively lead in educational institutions. Let's apply your knowledge to a case study that is representative of the challenges that transformational leaders regularly face. After reading the case study, respond to the prompts and reflect on your own decision-making pedagogy. Good luck!

A Case Study for Decision Making

The following is an excellent example of how a leader can be faced with overwhelming pressure to act in ways that may not be in the best interest of the institution. This realistic case study will illustrate how a high school principal is faced with a decision that is anything but easy. If the principal follows transformational decision-making guidelines and philosophy, the decision can be made with a clear conscience. After reading the details of this school case study within the context of your own past precedent, local policy, and applicable law, reflect on your own decision-making pedagogy and ask yourself what decision you would have made. Then, read the decision made by the principal and see if you agree or disagree.

It is now 4:00 p.m. on Wednesday afternoon and Principal Smith has been mulling over a high-profile discipline situation that includes the possible expulsion of three high school students, including a star football player with an exemplary academic reputation. This is the day Principal Smith promised to make a final decision on the course of action against the star athlete–student (Jim), his girlfriend (Michelle), and a sophomore boy (John), who lives two doors down from Jim in an affluent suburban neighborhood.

On the previous Monday morning, the students were seen smoking marijuana in the parking lot behind the school, beyond the range of school cameras. A teacher who walks to school occasionally came around the corner of a building in time to see all three students taking turns smoking the joint with their backs turned to the approaching teacher. As the teacher got within 30 feet of the three students, Jim, finally noticing the approaching teacher, hurriedly threw the half-inch-long butt on the ground and mashed what was left into the pavement beside his vehicle. The sophomore boy, being startled and scared, ran toward the student parking lot where other students were leaving their cars and entering the school. Jim and his girlfriend simply started walking toward the teacher, attempting to minimize what was becoming an obvious surprise bust. Jim walked up to the teacher, offered his hand, and introduced his girlfriend, Michelle, to the teacher. The teacher, Mrs. Konomos, remained calm and asked them what they had been doing. Jim and Michelle simultaneously said, "Nothing!" Mrs. Konomos told both students to accompany her to the school's administrative office. Almost instinctively, Mrs. Konomos asked the name of the student who had run from the scene. In the same breath, Mrs. Konomos asked why the other student had run if they were not doing anything. Jim replied that he did not know the student and that he had just walked up to them and handed them something. At that point, Mrs. Konomos walked both students into the school and asked them to proceed with her to the assistant principal's office. Reluctantly, both began walking with the teacher, asking her to please understand and not to report this to the principal. Jim even offered to do anything if the teacher would simply forget the whole ordeal. By this time, all three had arrived at the administrative offices of the school.

The assistant principal was given the details of what Mrs. Konomos had observed in the parking lot. The assistant principal instructed Mrs. Konomos to request the principal's assistance in seizing the evidence from the parking lot. Fortunately, there was enough evidence in the parking lot to officially determine that it was indeed marijuana. In the course of the investigation, Jim allowed the administrators to search his parents' car. Jim had driven to school in his parents' SUV. Under the seat, a small plastic bag was found containing a very small amount of marijuana. When confronted with all the evidence, both Jim and Michelle admitted to smoking marijuana. The sophomore boy, John, also was named, and he, too, admitted his part in the drug smoking that morning. The police were called, and they made a formal arrest of all three students. The three students were taken from the school to the police station. All three sets of parents were notified of the circumstances and asked to report to the police station. The superintendent was notified, who in turn notified the five-member school board of what had happened and who was involved.

At this point, it would seem a clear case of student drug use. All details of the investigation followed applicable school law procedures. All three students admitted their guilt when questioned, and all three tested positive for marijuana in their drug-testing samples. Seemingly, Principal Smith had only to determine what discipline should be administered. But Principal Smith has had numerous similar instances in his 24 years as an administrator. He knows full well that no decision on disciplining students is ever easy, particularly in cases of a high-profile nature, when community awareness is also high. All of these factors make the decision-making process agonizing for Principal Smith. Consider the following pressures to the decision-making process for Principal Smith.

The football team is undefeated and ranked number one in the state polls. State tournament action begins this Friday evening. The school has never won a football state championship. The union president, who also serves as the head football coach, is a student advocate who constantly criticizes the administration for how it runs the school. Jim's dad is the owner of a local steel fabrication company and a former NFL player. He is also president of the largest local service organization. Additionally, Jim's father is a jogging partner of the school board president. Both parents are supporting parent booster club members. Jim's mother was the national runner-up for the Junior Miss pageant 22 years earlier. Both parents are well embedded in the community and viewed as "hometown kids done well." Michelle, Jim's girlfriend, is a member of the cheerleading squad that had just won the state championship in cheerleading competition at the state fair 2 weeks earlier. Her mother and father are very supportive parents and have never called the school to complain about anything. Jim's mother is known for her protection of her children and has called many times in the past threatening legal action if the school did anything to jeopardize her son's education. Jim has had repeated school violations, including stealing food in the cafeteria, an alleged smoking incident in the school's restroom, and numerous tardies and absences beyond the allowable limit. Additionally, Jim has been sent to the office for disruptive classroom behavior. Jim had also been arrested for underage drinking at a party the previous spring that was raided by local police officers. Jim's parents were able to hire an attorney and have all charges dismissed. The third student, John, had no previous trouble either at school or with the police. His parents are divorced, and he is living with his father, who is also an attorney. The president of the school board already does not like the principal because of disciplinary action that Principal Smith took against his daughter 3 years earlier. The superintendent is usually supportive unless the decision is divisive or controversial. Many consider the superintendent a "good news" administrator who is not willing to tackle challenging issues. Very quickly, the superintendent is sending out vibes to be careful with this one. A bad decision might end the principal's tenure and force early retirement.

Given past precedent, local policy, and applicable law, Principal Smith is considering the following options:

1. Expel all three for 1 year.

2. Expel all three for a period of time less than 1 year.

3. Give all three students 10 days out of school and require all three to submit to random drug testing.

4. Let all three students back in school immediately with the understanding they are to enter a drug-counseling program with their parents. They further agree to random drug testing.

5. Simply give the students a short suspension out of school with the statement that it is a police matter and that the students will have enough punishment with the law and don't need further punishment from the school.

6. A combination of any and all of the above.

It is now time for the principal to make his final decision. Principal Smith is well schooled in using transformational decision making, having applied this pedagogy for many years. Following the principles of sound decision making, Principal Smith is in complete control of his decisions. He has consistently made decisions with a clear conscience and with the resolve that he is doing what is best for the common good of the school (institution). By maintaining a transformational focus, he is free of guilt and knows that ultimately, his final decision will be in the best interest of the students, too. What would you do?

The path to a decision was surprisingly easy. Mr. Smith expelled all three students for two semesters. The students were given the option to remove one semester from the expulsion if they agreed to attend six counseling sessions that included their parents. As a part of this agreement, the students agreed to random drug testing for 1 year. Jim and Michelle also were removed from their respective sports and were told they could not participate in any extracurricular activities until they returned to school in good standing. The sophomore boy, John, also was banned from any extracurricular activities until he returned to school in good standing. This was consistent with past practices and applicable laws.

Why was this the best decision for the institution (i.e., the school)?

1. It sent a strong message to the community, parents, students, and teachers that the school would not tolerate drugs at school. Any discipline decisions that were less severe might have seriously compromised the school's ability to function effectively.

2. It sent a strong message that decision making will not be influenced by who you are.

3. It sent a strong message that the integrity of the institutional common good is more important than any one individual in the institution.

4. The superintendent may not have agreed with the decisions, but a defining moment was created, and the superintendent hopefully supported the decision. The football coach may be devastated, wishing he could have his star player back, but he, too, will hopefully understand why the decision was made. The principal should use this experience as an opportunity to explain to the coach the decision-making process and pledge to support the coach as he makes the same tough decisions in the classroom and on the field.

5. Principal Smith hoped that the parents supported and understood the importance of the decision, but he recognized that they may not.

Summary

Transformational decision making was created to give leaders the confidence and empowerment to act decisively with a sound decision-making pedagogy. Leaders who embrace this pedagogy will find themselves leading in profoundly positive and meaningful ways with stakeholders benefiting as the vision, mission, and overall common good permeate decisions.

Transformational decision making was not designed to tell leaders what decisions to make, but rather how to make decisions by providing a framework of sound decision making. Simply stated, this pedagogy better ensures successful leadership by encouraging leaders to ask the question, "What is in the best interest of the institution I lead?" The genuine and thoughtful answer to this question requires a strong personal resolve, a persistent resilience to criticism, a powerful conviction of purpose, and a clear conscience.

Conceptual Framework

Transformational decision making is a framework of considerations to guide your leadership, not a rigid template professing decision-making answers. However, one question should be asked by all: "What is in the best interest of the institution I lead?" As you implement and lead in transforming ways, you can improve transformational effectiveness by considering the following:

1. Minimize worry about decisions. If the vision, mission, and common good are central to decisions, you can act with confidence.

2. Decision making can be lonely. Develop collegial and collaborative peer networks with others making institutional decisions.

3. Don't be afraid to fail. Failure may be an essential part of any educational institution reaching its potential.

4. Discipline at all institutional levels is healthy. Discipline communicates procedures and rules, encourages self-control, and articulates expectations. Discipline enhances decision making.

5. Decisions should be made at the lowest institutional level. Otherwise, stakeholder buy-in is marginalized.

Reflective Thinking

1. Difficult decisions can be fraught with negative feedback. How do you overcome this? What role do peer networks play in overcoming the loneliness associated with decision making?

2. Discipline can be conceptualized at the personal and institutional levels. Give examples of both personal and institutional discipline considered essential for decision making in your institution.

3. Do you practice the pedagogy of keeping decision making at the lowest level? What happens when decision making has strong oversight? What are the advantages and disadvantages of lowest-level decision making?

Resource

Decision Making
Self-Assessment

1. When I make difficult decisions in my role as a leader, I think about how the decision will affect my family or me.

E	D	C	B	A
Rarely	25% of the time	50% of the time	75% of the time	Usually

2. I believe that as a leader, I should hire people who will say positive things about me.

E	D	C	B	A
Rarely	25% of the time	50% of the time	75% of the time	Usually

3. When I make difficult decisions in my role as a leader, I gather as much objective data as necessary and make the decision based solidly on that input.

A	B	C	D	E
Rarely	25% of the time	50% of the time	75% of the time	Usually

4. When I make difficult decisions in my role as a leader, I am driven by a competitive spirit to win.

E	D	C	B	A
Rarely	25% of the time	50% of the time	75% of the time	Usually

5. When I make difficult decisions in my role as a leader, I normally think of the common good instead of what is good for individuals.

A	B	C	D	E
Rarely	25% of the time	50% of the time	75% of the time	Usually

6. I believe there might come a time when leading immorally is justified.

E	D	C	B	A
Rarely	25% of the time	50% of the time	75% of the time	Usually

7. When I make difficult decisions in my role as a leader, they negatively affect more than half the people affected by the decision.

A	B	C	D	E
Rarely	25% of the time	50% of the time	75% of the time	Usually

8. When I make difficult decisions in my role as a leader, I consider how the institution I lead will be affected by the decision.

A	B	C	D	E
Rarely	25% of the time	50% of the time	75% of the time	Usually

9. I believe that as a leader, test scores should drive decision making.

E	D	C	B	A
Rarely	25% of the time	50% of the time	75% of the time	Usually

10. I believe that change is inevitable in education, and it is my leadership duty to sell the importance of change to stakeholders of education.

E	D	C	B	A
Rarely	25% of the time	50% of the time	75% of the time	Usually

11. As a leader, I view everyone in the institution that I lead as equally important.

A	B	C	D	E
Rarely	25% of the time	50% of the time	75% of the time	Usually

12. I believe that if I sell a decision the right way, I can convince others that the decision is the proper one.

E	D	C	B	A
Rarely	25% of the time	50% of the time	75% of the time	Usually

13. I believe that it is not important to please my direct superior in my decision making.

E	D	C	B	A
Rarely	25% of the time	50% of the time	75% of the time	Usually

14. I believe that people are motivated by coercion or threats.

E	D	C	B	A
Rarely	25% of the time	50% of the time	75% of the time	Usually

15. When all things have been considered in the decision-making process and no decision is apparent, I use informed intuition to drive the decision one direction or another.

A	B	C	D	E
Rarely	25% of the time	50% of the time	75% of the time	Usually

16. I believe that any decision will work out for the best if I have faith in the decision.

E	D	C	B	A
Rarely	25% of the time	50% of the time	75% of the time	Usually

17. I believe that the end justifies the means when making decisions.

E	D	C	B	A
Rarely	25% of the time	50% of the time	75% of the time	Usually

18. If I were to lead a school with a direct superior who oversees everything I do, I would make a concerted effort to understand my boss's larger viewpoint when making decisions.

A	B	C	D	E
Rarely	25% of the time	50% of the time	75% of the time	Usually

19. I believe that emotions can provide valuable insight into proper decision making.

E	D	C	B	A
Rarely	25% of the time	50% of the time	75% of the time	Usually

20. I believe that a leader must have the resolve to make decisions decisively and in a timely manner, even if clear direction is lacking.

E	D	C	B	A
Rarely	25% of the time	50% of the time	75% of the time	Usually

21. I believe that students should serve as the core of all decision making in schools.

E	D	C	B	A
Rarely	25% of the time	50% of the time	75% of the time	Usually

22. I believe that individual people are motivated primarily by their physiological and psychological needs.

A	B	C	D	E
Rarely	25% of the time	50% of the time	75% of the time	Usually

23. I believe that a leader must have the liberty to manipulate or massage data to support a tough decision so that those affected by the decision will be convinced of the decision's efficacy.

E	D	C	B	A
Rarely	25% of the time	50% of the time	75% of the time	Usually

24. I believe that most decisions come from my gut feelings and are based on experience.

E	D	C	B	A
Rarely	25% of the time	50% of the time	75% of the time	Usually

25. I believe that there are times when a leader may be forced to do something somewhat illegal to justify difficult decisions.

E	D	C	B	A
Rarely	25% of the time	50% of the time	75% of the time	Usually

26. I believe that leaders with unhealthy addictions, such as drugs or alcohol, can continue to lead without serious consequences to their decision making if care is taken.

E	D	C	B	A
Rarely	25% of the time	50% of the time	75% of the time	Usually

27. If my immediate superior overrules a decision I have made because he or she says the decision is bad for the institution, I accept his or her decision.

A	B	C	D	E
Rarely	25% of the time	50% of the time	75% of the time	Usually

28. I believe that it is natural for schools or school districts to use competition as a means for improvement.

E	D	C	B	A
Rarely	25% of the time	50% of the time	75% of the time	Usually

29. I believe that offering extrinsic incentives, such as money, for doing a good job best motivates people.

E	D	C	B	A
Rarely	25% of the time	50% of the time	75% of the time	Usually

30. I believe that there are powerful outside forces that will ultimately dictate the most important decisions needing to be made, thus making the leader a relatively unimportant part of the decision-making process.

E	D	C	B	A
Rarely	25% of the time	50% of the time	75% of the time	Usually

31. I believe that I rarely make bad decisions because I am usually right about what direction the institution must take, given my innate and historical leadership ability.

E	D	C	B	A
Rarely	25% of the time	50% of the time	75% of the time	Usually

32. I believe that a leader should be driven to leave a legacy of leadership.

E	D	C	B	A
Rarely	25% of the time	50% of the time	75% of the time	Usually

33. I believe that the institution's vision and mission serve as the core of decision making.

A	B	C	D	E
Rarely	25% of the time	50% of the time	75% of the time	Usually

34. I believe that people are the most important consideration when making decisions.

E	D	C	B	A
Rarely	25% of the time	50% of the time	75% of the time	Usually

35. I believe that when decisions are made to improve education in our schools, competition is more effective than collaboration.

E	D	C	B	A
Rarely	25% of the time	50% of the time	75% of the time	Usually

36. I believe that a leader's professional dress will be a highly effective way to build respect for the leader.

E	D	C	B	A
Rarely	25% of the time	50% of the time	75% of the time	Usually

37. When I make tough decisions in my role as a leader that involve resources such as money, my primary focus is improved test scores.

E	D	C	B	A
Rarely	25% of the time	50% of the time	75% of the time	Usually

38. I believe that there are times a leader must consider acting unethically to ensure that the institution he or she serves is furthered.

E	D	C	B	A
Rarely	25% of the time	50% of the time	75% of the time	Usually

39. I believe that it is a primary role of individuals being led to please their leader.

E	D	C	B	A
Rarely	25% of the time	50% of the time	75% of the time	Usually

40. When difficult decisions have to be made, a large consideration must include how those affected will accept the decision.

E	D	C	B	A
Rarely	25% of the time	50% of the time	75% of the time	Usually

Scoring: Count the total number of each LETTER you marked for all 40 questions and then multiply that number by the factor listed below for each LETTER to tally a score for each LETTER. Add the tallied scores for each LETTER to get a total composite score.

A = 1
B = 2
C = 3
D = 4
E = 5

For example: 40 total questions might be broken down as follows:

4 statements were marked	A	$4 \times 1 = 4$
8 statements were marked	B	$8 \times 2 = 16$
7 statements were marked	C	$7 \times 3 = 21$
12 statements were marked	D	$12 \times 4 = 48$
9 statements were marked	E	$9 \times 5 = 45$

TOTAL COMPOSITE SCORE   134

SCORING EXPLANATION:

Scores between 200 and 148 indicate that you are doing a good job of leading using a sound decision-making pedagogy. This book will confirm your leadership decision-making abilities.

Scores between 144 and 92 indicate that you have not fully embraced an effective decision-making pedagogy, and this book will further your leadership decision-making abilities.

Scores between 91 and 40 indicate that you have not embraced a sound decision-making pedagogy, and this book could transform your leadership decision-making abilities.

Bibliography

Barth, R. S. (1990). *Improving schools from within.* San Francisco: Jossey-Bass.

Bast, J. L., & Walberg, H. J. (2003). *Education and capitalism.* Stanford, CA: Hoover.

Beck, U. (1998). The cosmopolitan manifesto. *New Statesman, 11*(496), 28–30.

Blanchard, K. (1999). *The heart of the leader.* Tulsa, OK: Honor Books.

Blanchard, K., Hodges, P., & Hybels, B. (1999). *Leadership by the book.* New York: Morrow.

Blanchard, K., & Johnson, S. (1981). *The one-minute manager.* New York: Berkley.

Bosso, C. J. (1994). The contextual bases of problem definition. In *The politics of problem definition* (pp. 182–203). Lawrence: University Press of Kansas.

Brower, R., & Balch, B. (2004). The eleven fundamental laws of human nature and their influence on decision-making. *The Journal, 50*(2), 17–20.

Cooper, B. S., Fusarelli, L. D., & Randall, E. V. (2004). *Better policies, better schools: Theories and applications.* Boston: Pearson.

Cottrill, K. (2002). Racing uncertainty. *Traffic World, 266*(48), 18.

Covey, S. (1990). *Principle-centered leadership.* New York: Simon & Schuster.

Cox, D. (1992). *Leadership when the heat's on.* New York: McGraw-Hill.

Deming, E. (1986). *Out of crisis.* Cambridge: MIT Center for Advanced Engineering Study.

Dore, A. (1995, April). "Me First" society set to come second. *The Times Educational Supplement,* p. 3.

Drucker, P. (1954). *The practice of management.* New York: Harper & Row.

Drucker, P. (1974). *Management: Tasks, practices, responsibilities.* New York: HarperCollins.

Drucker, P. (1990). *Managing the non-profit organization.* New York: HarperCollins.

Fullan, M. (1991). *The new meaning of educational change.* New York: Teachers College Press.

Fullan, M. (1993). *Change forces.* Bristol, PA: Falmer.

Gardner, J. (1990). *On leadership.* New York: Free Press.

Glasser, W. (1986). *Control theory in the classroom.* New York: Harper & Row.

Glasser, W. (1998). *Choice theory.* New York: HarperCollins.

Glickman, C. D. (1993). *Renewing America's schools.* San Francisco: Jossey-Bass.

Goodlad, J. I. (1997). *The public purpose of education and schooling.* San Francisco: Jossey-Bass.

Goodwyn, L. (1978). *The populist movement: A short history of the agrarian revolt in America.* Oxford, UK: Oxford University Press.

Gray, D. (2000). Shaping America's workforce for the new millennium. *Education, 120*(4), 631–633.

Hersey, P., & Blanchard, K. (1982). *Management of human behavior: Utilizing human resources.* Englewood Cliffs, NJ: Prentice Hall.

Herzberg, F. (1966). *Work and the nature of man.* New York: World.

Ip, G. (2002, October 24). The economy: Fed chief is encouraged by productivity growth. *Wall Street Journal,* p. A2.

Kleinginna, P. R., & Kleinginna, A. M. (1981). A categorized list of motivation definitions, with a suggestion for a consensual definition. *Motivation and Emotion, 5*(3), 263–291.

Krashen, S. (1993). *The power of reading.* Englewood, CO: Libraries Unlimited.

LeBoeuf, M. (1979). *Working smart: How to accomplish more in half the time.* New York: Warner.

Machiavelli, N. (1952). *The prince.* New York: Mentor Classic-New American Library.

Maiello, M. (2002). They almost changed the world. *Forbes, 170*(13), 217.

Martin, W. J., & Willower, D. J. (1981). The managerial behavior of high school principals. *Educational Administration Quarterly, 17,* 69–90.

Maslow, A. (1954). *Motivation and personality.* New York: Basic Books.

McGregor, D. (1960). *The human side of enterprise.* New York: McGraw-Hill.

Miel, A. (1996, Summer). Curriculum that matters: Visions of what ought to be. *Educational Forum, 60,* 340.

Milstein, M., & Farkas, J. (1988). The over-stated case of educator stress. *Journal of Educational Administration, 26*(2), 232–249.

National Commission on Excellence in Education. (1983). *A nation at risk: The imperative for educational reform.* Washington, DC: U.S. Government Printing Office.

Peters, T., & Waterman, R. (1982). *In pursuit of excellence: Lessons from America's best-run companies.* New York: HarperCollins.

Peters, T. (1987). *Thriving on chaos.* New York: Harper & Row.

Peters, T. (1994). *The pursuit of WOW.* New York: Vantage.

Prestine, N. A., & McGreal, T. L. (1997). Fragile changes, sturdy lives: Implementing authentic assessment in schools. *Educational Administration Quarterly, 33*(3), 371–400.

Prior, M. (2003). Meeting the needs of the me generation. *DSN Retailing Today, 42*(23), 22.

Reindl, T. (2004). A wake-up call for a world leader. *College and University, 79*(4), 33–34.

Schlechty, P. (1997). *Inventing better schools.* San Francisco: Jossey-Bass.

Senge, P. (1990). *The fifth discipline.* New York: Doubleday.

Sergiovanni, T. (1999). *Rethinking leadership.* Arlington Heights, IL: Skylight Training and Publishing.

Skinner, B. F. (1953). *Science and human behavior.* New York: Macmillan.

Stedman, L., & Kaestle, C. (1987). Literacy and reading performance in the United States from 1880 to the present. *Reading Research Quarterly, 22,* 59–78.

Stipek, D. (1988). *Motivation to learn: From theory to practice.* Englewood Cliffs, NJ: Prentice Hall.

Stogdill, R. (1959). *Individual behavior and group achievement.* New York: Oxford University Press.

Wexler, B. (2003). Poetry is dead. Does anybody really care? *Newsweek, 141*(18), 18.

Wheatley, M. (1992). *Leadership and the new science: Learning about organizations from an orderly universe.* San Francisco: Berrett-Koehler.

Wilson, B. L., & Rossman, G. B. (1993). *Mandating academic excellence: High school responses to state curriculum reform.* New York: Teachers College Press.

Index

**CORWIN
PRESS**

The Corwin Press logo—a raven striding across an open book—represents the union of courage and learning. Corwin Press is committed to improving education for all learners by publishing books and other professional development resources for those serving the field of K–12 education. By providing practical, hands-on materials, Corwin Press continues to carry out the promise of its motto: **"Helping Educators Do Their Work Better."**